Francis L. Patton

The Inspiration of the Scriptures

Francis L. Patton

The Inspiration of the Scriptures

ISBN/EAN: 9783337183424

Printed in Europe, USA, Canada, Australia, Japan

Cover: Foto ©ninafisch / pixelio.de

More available books at **www.hansebooks.com**

THE

INSPIRATION

OF

THE SCRIPTURES.

BY THE
REV. FRANCIS L. PATTON, D.D.

PHILADELPHIA:
PRESBYTERIAN BOARD OF PUBLICATION,
No. 1334 CHESTNUT STREET.

PREFACE.

It is the writer's hope that this attempt to indicate the steps by which we are led to the sure position that the Scriptures are an infallible guide, may aid the faith of some who belong to that increasing class of men who are disposed to speak with hesitancy concerning the divine authorship of the Bible.

Nyack on the Hudson, May 19, 1869.

CONTENTS.

CHAPTER I.

THE SCRIPTURES ARE TRUSTWORTHY.

                                      PAGE

Introductory—Divine Authority of the Bible an Important Question at the Present Time—Bible a Series of Literary Documents—Their Historical Credibility—Authorship of the Pentateuch—Profane History Confirmatory of Scripture—Rawlinson Quoted—False Theories concerning the Person of Christ Refuted by Establishing the Historic Credibility of the Gospels—Christianity does not depend on the Doctrine of Inspiration—The Argument *a fortiori*........ 9

CHAPTER II.

THE BIBLE CONTAINS THE WORD OF GOD.

The Scriptures Speak for themselves—No Fallacy in Arguing from their Credibility to their Inspiration—Supernatural Element in Scripture: (1.) Miracles; (2.) Recital of Divine Communications; (3.) Predictions: these not Written after the Events Occurred; not Analogous to Heathen Prognostications; not Instances of Farsighted Sagacity, but Divine

Utterances—hence their Evidential Value; (4.) Doctrines which must have been Revealed, as we know (*a*) from their Inherent Excellence, (*b*) their Adaptation to Human Wants, (*c*) the Mysteriousness of Some, (*d*) the Apparent Irreconcilability of Others—Bible Contains the Word of God........ 24

CHAPTER III.

The Whole Bible is God's Message.

Difference between a True and an Official Account—Bible is an Authoritative Expression of God's Will—This shown (1) by the Official Rank of the Writers; (2.) The Bible is the only Account of the Way of Salvation; (3.) It is Pervaded by one Purpose; (4.) Relation in which the Historical Portions stand to rest of Scripture; (5.) Direct Testimony of Bible 41

CHAPTER IV.

Divine Agency Employed in the Composition of Scripture.

Is the Bible a Human or Divine Account of Supernatural Revelations?—The fact that the Bible is God's Message raises a Presumption in Favor of its Infallibility—This Presumption sustained by Several Considerations: (1.) Extended Account of Divine Communications; (2.) Marvellous Accuracy of Scripture; (3.) Motives ascribed to Men and Reasons assigned for Divine Acts by the Writers of Scripture; (4.) Reticence of the Writers and their Wisdom in Selection of Facts; (5.) Relations subsisting between the Several Books of the New Testament............................... 53

CONTENTS.

CHAPTER V.

PLENARY INSPIRATION.

PAGE

Do Scriptures teach Plenary or Partial Inspiration?—Plenary Inspiration of Old Testament proved: (1.) Names applied to Old Testament by Writers of the New; (2.) Deference paid to Old Testament; (3.) Its Infallibility asserted by the Saviour; (4.) Verbal References to Old Testament; (5.) Direct Assertions of Divine Authorship.—Arguments for Inspiration of New Testament................................. 72

CHAPTER VI.

OBJECTIONS CONSIDERED.

Spirit of Controversy at the Present Day Rationalistic—Objections to Plenary Inspiration: Obj. 1. Revelation said to be Impossible—Objection rests on False Philosophy; Obj. 2. Bible said to Contradict Science—Scripture, though not Technical, teaches no Error; Obj. 3. Bible said to Contradict Itself—Conflicting Passages examined; Obj. 4. Unimportant Passages; Obj. 5 based on 1 Cor. chap. vii.—Lee quoted—Proof demanded for Theory of Partial Inspiration—The Verifying Faculty—Office of Reason in Determining what is a Revelation................................. 93

CHAPTER VII.

EXPLICATION OF THE DOCTRINE.

(1.) Inspiration covers only the Original MSS.—Importance of this Remark—Have we a Correct Text?—Professor Stuart quoted—Difference between an Inspired and Uninspired Original. (2.) No Inspiration claimed for Writers of Scripture Outside of their Official Work—Infallibility as Authors did not make them Faultless as Men. (3.) Agency of Spirit in making Sacred Writers Infallible not equivalent to his Sanctifying Grace—Confusion arising out of applying same name to Both—Mistake of Maurice. (4.) Inspiration, though Verbal, is not Mechanical—Dr. Bannerman Quoted and Reviewed. (5.) There is a Difference Between Revelation and Inspiration—Does Inspiration imply Revelation?—Controversy between Dr. Lee and Dr. Bannerman alluded to—Revelation Defined. (6.) There is a Human and a Divine Element in Scripture.............. 112

THE INSPIRATION OF THE SCRIPTURES.

CHAPTER I.

THE SCRIPTURES ARE TRUSTWORTHY.

THE Bible is the sole warrant for the existence of the Christian society. The facts on which the Christian system is based, and the doctrines which constitute that system, are authoritatively recorded nowhere else.

The members of this society agree in ascribing divine honours to Jesus. They trust him as their Saviour. They observe religiously the day which commemorates his resurrection. They recognize obligations which do not fall within the circle of duty described by human ethics. They foster hopes which can be realized only in a future world.

If the Bible is not true, they are entertaining beliefs which have not a shadow of support—are forming plans in which they must meet with bitter disappointment. The Christian is resting the fortunes of his soul on the authority of the book which he calls the Bible. He is contented to settle the question of his destiny by complying with the directions which are offered him in its pages.

It cannot, therefore, be a matter of mere literary curiosity to inquire into the reasons for receiving this book. The thinking Christian must feel a desire to know why he is required to take it as his rule of faith.

Nor will it do to say that the question concerning the divine authority of the Bible has been settled, and there is no need of bringing it up for fresh discussion. It is a subject of vital interest at the present day. Opposition to the doctrine of the infallibility of the Scriptures comes from a quarter which makes it more injurious in its effects. The spirit of Rationalism has invaded the Church, and among professing Christians, and even Christian ministers, there are only too many who adopt loose views on this fundamental question, and give utterance to sentiments which are seriously damaging to the faith of God's people.

If, as it is claimed, the Bible is the word of God, and if the writers in the words they used acted under the guidance of the Holy Ghost, it is fair to suppose that the argument can be presented in a way which will satisfy the minds of those who are inquiring on the subject. If the doctrine of inspiration is one which claims our faith, there must be evidence for it.

I shall endeavour in the following pages to indicate the steps by which we are led to a definite statement concerning the authorship of the Bible. The discussion will take the shape of an inquiry rather than a defence. I shall approach the subject not as the advocate of any particular theory of inspiration, but as one desirous of learning all that the Bible can tell me concerning the agency employed in its composition. The conclusions which are reached will be the result of an inductive investigation.

The Bible comes into the hands of the student as a series of literary documents. It would be premature at this stage of our inquiries to attach much importance to the claim which they make of being a revelation from God. The question of their historic credibility must first be settled according to the rules of historical criticism. It is fair for the inquirer to ask whether these documents are reliable. Can we trust them as the vehicles of historical information? Is the Pentateuch, for example, the production of its reputed author, or is it a forgery which was palmed upon the Hebrew people? These are questions of vital importance. The discussion of them belongs to the department of theology known as Introduction. The reader must refer to the works of such writers as Horne, Havernick, Jahn, Rawlinson, etc., if he wishes to see how the arguments of those who assail the credibility of the Scriptures have been met, and how completely the Bible has been vindicated.

Little more is possible here than the statement that the books of the Old and New Testaments have been subjected to the most thorough critical handling, and that their credibility as historic documents has been placed beyond dispute. Better evidence of their authenticity we could not have than is furnished in the fact that they have passed safely through the ordeal of German criticism.

No objection has been raised against the genuineness and authenticity of the Pentateuch sufficiently grave to outweigh the testimony of the entire Jewish nation. The study of the Old Testament will show that the Jews as early as the reign of David were confident that Moses wrote the first five books of the Scriptures. So deeply was this conviction rooted in the national mind that political differences, even when they culminated in schisms, were not strong enough to induce either party to cast discredit on the books which bear the name of their lawgiver. Though the Pentateuch was the statute-book of Judah, the ten tribes showed no disposition to set aside its authority, as we learn from the fact that the Samaritans received it alone of all the Old Testament Scriptures, because it was the book of the Law given by Moses. It has, indeed, been alleged that writing was not known in the time of Moses, or, if known, that writing materials were not at hand adapted for so large a work under the circumstances of a wilderness journey. This objection, however, has been set aside by recent discoveries of Babylonian bricks and Egyptian papyruses, which are estimated to be coeval with Moses. "It has been said that if Moses had written the book, he would not have spoken of himself in the third person, and that he would not have applied to himself terms of praise and expressions of honour."* To which it is enough to reply by saying that parallel passages may be cited from the writings of Homer and Chaucer, of Cæsar and Xenophon, and even of the Apostle Paul. These are considerations which abundantly confirm the testimony of

* Rawlinson's Historical Evidences, p 52.

the Hebrew people. That a deliberate forgery could have won the confidence of the nation so as to have been regarded by them in the light of a sacred trust, embodying their history, their genealogies, their laws and their religious institutions, is a supposition which cannot be entertained. Yet the book must have been written by Moses, or be the work of an impostor. That Moses was the author of the books attributed to him is evident from the fact that they were written by one who was an eye-witness of most of the events recorded. The careful attention which the writer bestows upon the record of places, battles, marches, etc., the minute circumstances which he weaves into the narrative, corroborate the belief that he was a participator in the transactions, and that he wrote from personal knowledge.

The books were evidently written while the events were in progress. There is no systematic division of the material into subjects, as would be the case to a greater or less extent with a historian writing from reflection or crystallizing floating traditions. Historical facts, laws, admonitions follow each other without any other relation than that of chronological sequence. They were written in the form of a journal, and by one who knew whereof he affirmed. The use of archaic forms of expression and of words of Egyptian origin, the allusions to the government and social life of the Egyptians—particularly the mention of their practice of embalming the dead—prove that the writer must have lived in a time as early as Moses, and must have enjoyed a familiarity with foreign customs which is best explained by the circumstances attending the education and early life of the Jewish lawgiver. Finally, the distinct declarations that God commanded Moses to write the discomfiture of Amalek in a book—that Moses wrote all the words of the Law, and took the book of the covenant and read it in the audience of the people—that he made an end of writing the words of the Law in a book till they were finished, and bade the Levites who bare the ark of the covenant take that book of the Law and put it in the side of the ark of the covenant of the Lord, that it might be there for a witness against the people—leave no room for doubt that Moses was the author of the books which bear his name. This, it is conceded by our opponents, is enough to settle the veracity of the narrative. "It would most unquestionably," says Strauss, "be an argument of *decisive* weight in favour of the credibility of the biblical history could it indeed be shown that it was written by eye-witnesses."*

The historical books which follow, though of uncertain authorship are nevertheless, authentic, as both internal and external evidence abundantly testify. They have the "force of state papers, being the authoritative public documents, preserved among the national archives of the Jews, so long as they were a nation; and ever since cherished by the scattered fragments of the race as among the most precious of their early records."†

We are, however, more than compensated for their anonymous character by the abundant corroborative testimony which these books receive from other portions of Scripture and from profane sources. Kings and Chronicles are independent records, and, so far as they cover common ground, serve to substantiate each other. The historical books of the Old Testament receive an endorsement in the writings of the prophets analogous to that which the book of Acts receives in the Epistles of Paul. The reader may verify this by comparing the prophecies of Isaiah with the second book of Kings—for example, the accounts of the sickness of Hezekiah

* Quoted by Rawlinson, Hist'l. Ev. p. 57.
† Rawlinson, p. 80.

and the death of Sennacherib (Isa. xxxvii. 8; 2 Kings xix. 20). Recent antiquarian and historical studies have thrown light upon the Scriptures. The "giant cities of Bashan" of which Moses tells us, no longer afford opportunity for a jest at the expense of Scripture. They still exist, the silent but enduring monuments to the veracity of the Hebrew historian.* Scientific inquiries confirm the Bible accounts of the creation, the origin of man, the unity of the race and the ethnic relations of mankind. "The *Toldoth Beni Noah*," says Rawlinson, "has extorted the admiration of modern ethnologists, who continually find in it anticipations of their greatest discoveries." Archæological researches in Nineveh and Babylon illustrate the state of art in the age of Solomon among the nations contiguous to the Jews, and among other things remove the

* "At least a thousand square miles of Og's ancient kingdom were spread out before me. There was the country whose giant (Rephaim, Gen. xiv.) inhabitants the Eastern kings smote before they descended into the plains of Sodom. There were those threescore great cities of Argob whose walls and gates and brazen bars were noted with surprise by Moses and the Israelites, and whose Cyclopean architecture and massive stone gates even now fill the Western traveller with amazement, and give his simplest descriptions much of the charm and strangeness of Romance."—*Porter's Giant Cities of Bashan*, p. 30.

difficulty which the modern reader experiences in the Scripture account of the lavish use of gold for purposes of ornamentation, by showing that this was in accordance with the customs of the age.*

The Scripture accounts of the Assyrian monarchs who played an important part in the history of the Jews have in great measure been confirmed by Assyrian records. Of this a good illustration is the account of the invasion of Sennacherib, which we find minutely recorded in his annals as well as in the Bible. Assyrian monuments have come to the aid of the Christian student, and have reconciled the seeming contradiction between Daniel and Berosus, by giving a royal title to Belshazzar.†

Rawlinson thus sums up the result of the in-

---

* Rawlinson's Historical Evidences, p. 71.

† The account of the capture of Babylon by the Persians used to be cited as one of the cases where Scripture contradicts profane history. According to Daniel, the king *Belshazzar* was *killed* at the taking of Babylon. According to Berosus, the king *Nabonadius* was absent from the city at the time of its capture, and was afterward *treated with clemency*. A double contradiction! It was only in 1854 that Sir H. Rawlinson solved this difficulty by the discovery that Nabonadius had a son named Bil-sha-ruzer (Belshazzar), who had been associated with him in the government, and who shared the royal title. See Rawlinson, p. 139, and note p. 353.

vestigations which concern the authenticity of the Old Testament: "It has, I believe, been shown, in the first place, that the sacred narrative itself is the production of eye-witnesses, and therefore that it is entitled to the acceptance of all those who regard contemporary testimony as the main ground of all authentic history. And it has, secondly, been made apparent that all the evidence which we possess from profane sources of a really important and trustworthy character tends to confirm the truth of the history delivered to us in the sacred volume. The monumental records of past ages, Assyrian, Babylonian, Egyptian, Persian, Phœnician—the writings of historians who had based their histories on contemporary annals, as Manetho, Berosus, Dius, Menander, Nicolas of Damascus—the descriptions given by eye-witnesses of the Oriental manners and customs—the proofs obtained by modern research of the condition of art in the time and country—all combine to confirm, illustrate and establish the veracity of the writers who have delivered to us in the Pentateuch, in Joshua, Judges, Samuel, Kings and Chronicles, Ezra, Esther and Nehemiah, the history of the chosen people."

The students of Scripture have been equally successful in vindicating the historical credibility of the several books of the New Testament. What has been said will be sufficient to indicate the principles which guide investigation on this subject.

Before we prosecute our inquiries farther, let us notice the great advantage we have already gained. Take, for illustration, the case of the four evangegelists. If it can be established that the Gospels were written by those whose names they bear, it will be impossible to evade the statements which we find in them. It will not do to resort to *imposture* on the part of either Christ or his apostles in explanation of Christianity. The theory that the world has been duped and Judaism overthrown by a Galilean impostor never had plausibility enough to gain credence. The *statement* of the hypothesis that the disciples renounced their educational beliefs, and went forth to die in the attempt to propagate a deception, is its best refutation.

Equally unsatisfactory is the supposition that the men who for three years were the companions of Jesus could have been deceived when such abundant opportunities were afforded them of testing his claim to divine commission. The theory of *imposture* and of *self-deception* have both been tried and found wanting, and the enemies of Christianity have attempted to destroy the credibility of the Gospels by fixing on the second or third century as the time of their composition. But the *legendary* hypothesis cannot stand the test of historical criticism. It has been proved by an array of patristic testimony that the Gospels in their present form were read, quoted and received as authoritative by the Church early in the second century. In other words, we are left without the shadow of a doubt that these writings are the productions of their reputed authors.

This being the case, it follows that the character portrayed by the evangelists is that of a real man; that Jesus uttered the words attributed to him; that he gave signal proofs of his divinity, and wrought miracles in attestation of his divine commission. We learn, moreover, that the books of the Old Testament—held sacred by the Jews from time immemorial, though containing the record of their national crimes—were authoritatively endorsed by the Son of God. So when the credibility of the book of Acts is established, we prove that the apostles agreed in recognizing Jesus as the Messiah, and that they went forth amid dangers to preach the doctrine of the Resurrection; nay, that in Jerusalem, the very place where the enmity of the human heart had curdled into Pharisaic spite, they proclaimed that the "same Jesus, whom by wicked hands they had crucified and slain, God had raised from the dead."

If we could do no more than establish the historical credibility of the Bible, there would be evidence sufficient to condemn those who refuse to believe it. I must take exception to the disposition on the part of some to stake the fortunes of Christianity on the doctrine of Inspiration. Not that I yield to any one in profound conviction of the truth and importance of this doctrine. But it is proper for us to bear in mind the immense argumentative advantage which Christianity has, aside altogether from the inspiration of the documents on which it rests. I cannot agree with a recent writer when he says: "If we take away the inspired character of the Scripture narrative, we really shall possess little more certainty with regard to the facts of our Lord's life than we do to the facts of ancient Roman history. That this is not too strong a statement of the case is shown in the results of denying the inspired authority of the evangelists, as illustrated in romances which Strauss and Renan have proposed to substitute for the sacred history."*

* Garbett, God's Word Written, p. 330.

This passage, though occurring in a very able treatise on the subject of Inspiration, I cannot but look upon as too great a concession to the cause of Rationalism. The Christian apologist cannot meet infidel objections by assuming the doctrine of Inspiration. While the question of historical credibility is at issue, the battle must be fought on the ground of historical evidence. The romances of Strauss and Renan are triumphantly answered by proving the early origin of the Gospels. The Christian minister and apologist must never deprive himself of the argument *a fortiori* which is furnished him in the study of the Scriptures.

If on simple historical testimony it can be proved that Jesus wrought miracles, uttered prophecies and proclaimed his divinity—if it can be shown that he was crucified to redeem sinners, that he rose again from the dead, and that he made the destiny of men to hinge on their acceptance of him as their Saviour—then, whether the records which contain these truths be inspired or not, woe unto him who " neglects so great salvation!"

CHAPTER II.

THE BIBLE CONTAINS THE WORD OF GOD.

HAVING reached the position that the Scriptures are reliable, we are prepared to admit their testimony concerning themselves. They are competent witnesses concerning their own origin; and there is no fallacy involved in arguing from the credibility of the Bible to its inspiration. An objection is sometimes put in this form: "You must believe that the Bible is true before you can accept its testimony concerning its inspiration; and you must know that it is inspired before you can rely upon its statements. A circle evidently!" The difficulty is easily removed. Ordinary historical evidence is sufficient to satisfy us with regard to the truthfulness of statements which we find in the writings of Tacitus, Cæsar, Grote, Gibbon and Macaulay. We do not insist upon inspiration on the part of these authors as a guarantee of their credibility. Their books may contain errors. Instances of false reasoning, hasty generalization, incorrect judgment may occur in their pages, but of their *general truthfulness* we have no doubt. Historical criticism places the Bible on a level with the most reliable human histories. If, on after study, we find that the style in which the Scriptures are written, the information they contain, the harmony which pervades them indicate that supernatural agency was employed in their composition; if, moreover, the writers claim to have been guided by divine wisdom; if, by their references to the several books of the Bible, they indicate their conviction that the words of Scripture are the words of God,—then we are able to draw an inference far in advance of the general credibility of the Bible. We prove that, owing to the divine agency employed in its composition, it must be free from all mistakes incident to merely human authorship—that it can contain no errors in judgment, no inaccuracies in doctrinal statement. In short, from its credibility as a literary document we advance to its infallibility as God's message to men for the guidance of life.

At the threshold of our investigations into the contents of Scripture we are brought face to face with the supernatural. The Bible contains the account of God's miraculous presence in the affairs of human history; and this account is so closely woven into the texture of Scripture that its truthfulness cannot be invalidated without overthrowing all historical testimony. So that, whether the Bible is a supernatural production or not, it certainly does constitute in its main features a record of divine communications.

To illustrate this idea is the object of the present chapter.

(1.) *The Bible contains the account of miracles.*

We cannot deal with the miracles of Scripture as with the myths of ancient Greece and Rome, for the simple reason that instead of being the legends of a pre-historic age, they are matters of sober, well-authenticated fact, and constitute a very important part of the historic life of the Hebrew people. To show this, it is enough to mention the miracles which attested the divine commission of Moses and of his successors. Beginning with the plagues, we have the destruction of the first-born in Egypt, the passage of the Red Sea, the quails, the manna, the leprosy of Miriam, the judgment of Korah, Dathan and Abiram, the blossoming of Aaron's rod, the smiting of the rock at Meribah, the brazen serpent.

Then, the passage of the Jordan, the destruction

of Jericho, the defeat of the Gibeonites. Later still, the accounts of Elijah fed by ravens, the widow's cruse, Elijah's translation, the Shunamite's child, the cure of Naaman. And finally we have the well-authenticated accounts of the miracles of our Lord and his apostles.

We cannot separate miracles from their historical associations. The Bible presents the supernatural in the sphere of historical relations, and subjects it to the test of historical criticism. And the study of the Scriptures impresses upon us the conviction that the history which it embodies is a miraculous history—a history which has been shaped by divine agency.

(2.) *Many passages in the Bible claim to be the recital of divine communications.*

It is not strange that men whose ideas of history are cast in the mould of a naturalistic philosophy should try to break down the credibility of the Bible; for it contains a history in which the visible appearance of the divine Being and the audible utterance of divine communications are cardinal facts. Every institution which is characteristic of the Jewish people is wedded to the supernatural. Take, for example, the account of God's appearance to Moses when he kept the flocks of Jethro in

Horeb, of Moses' appointment to the leadership of Israel, of the institution of the Passover, of the deliverance of the Law in Sinai. These are salient points in Hebrew history, but they are linked with the utterance of divine communications. The Levitical code is the axis on which the civil, social and religious life of the Jews revolve, but it too came from the lips of Jehovah. The minute instructions concerning the ark, the altar, the tabernacle, the sacred vestments, the Urim and Thummim, the anointing oil, the consecration of the priests, were oral communications addressed to Moses. The laws concerning the sin, meat, burnt and trespass-offerings, the feast of tabernacles and the year of jubilee, find their explanation in the opening verse of the twentieth chapter of Exodus: "And God spake all these words."

The successor of Moses conducted his administration under the oral instructions of Jehovah. He crossed the Jordan, besieged Jericho, took Ai, divided the land, appointed cities of refuge, in accordance with divine direction.

The solemn preface with which the prophet always announced his message proves that he acted as the mouthpiece of God. Thus we read: "The word that Isaiah the son of Amoz saw concerning

Judah and Jerusalem;" "Thus saith the Lord;" "The word that came unto Jeremiah from the Lord, saying;" "Hear ye the word which the Lord speaketh to you, O house of Israel;" "And the word of the Lord came unto me saying, Son of man;" "Also, thou son of man, thus saith the Lord God unto the land of Israel," etc.

It is evident that if we should take out of Scripture all those portions which claim to relate what God said, we should rob the Bible of a large part of its contents. And if we should set aside all the historical facts which depend upon the oral utterances of God for their explanation, very little would be left worth calling history at all.

(3.) *The Bible contains predictions, together with the record of their fulfilment.*

God holds the key which unlocks the secrets of the centuries to come. We cannot dip into the future. The keenest foresight will not enable a man to write the history of the next year in advance. The elements which enter into the life of a nation are too numerous, the causes which operate on communities are too subtle, the motives which influence human conduct too inscrutable, for history ever to become a matter of prevision. The human will is an effectual barrier to the ambition of those who would carry scientific induction into the sphere of mind and make history a matter of calculation. Whatever may be the solution of the great question of the ages regarding the will, certain it is that so far as man is concerned the future must always be contingent, since the human spirit is either free, or the secret of its action is hid with Him who gave it being. Hence the predictive element of Scripture has always and deservedly held a position of high evidential importance. This element is a marked feature of the Bible. The destruction of Sennacherib, the death of Jezebel, the recovery of Hezekiah, the Babylonish captivity, the desolation of Edom, the fall of Babylon, the humbling of Egypt, the coming of the Messiah, the destruction of Jerusalem, are instances of fulfilled predictions which confront the denier of the supernatural.

It would be an easy way of disposing of these troublesome facts if the opponents of Revelation could say of them all, as of some they have the effrontery to say, that the so-called predictions were not written till the corresponding events had occurred. But God has taken care to put us in possession of evidence that the greater portion of the prophetic series was on record at the time of the

Babylonish captivity, and that therefore the predictions which concern Edom, Moab, the Philistines, Egypt, Babylon and the coming of Christ, antedate by centuries the events which constitute their accomplishment.

Nor is the cause of Rationalism helped by the appeal which is sometimes made to two or three cases of heathen prognostications. The saying of Seneca,* that the time would come when Shetland would cease to be the boundary of the known world, is adduced sometimes as a parallel to the prophecies of Scripture. As if the vague guesses of heathenism were at all analogous to the collection of definite predictions which we find in the Bible! The reader must remember that the contrast between Bible predictions and heathen oracles is not alone in the fact that the former are more discriminating and unambiguous, but also that instead of consisting of sporadic cases of prognostication, they constitute a collective series. "The evidence of prophecy," says Fairbairn, "is essentially of a connective and cumulative character. It does not consist so much in the verifications given to a few remarkable predictions, as in the establishment of an entire series closely related

* See Fairbairn on Prophecy, p. 207, American edition.

to each other, and forming a united and comprehensive whole." *

Let the reader study the series of prophetic utterances concerning the Jewish people and the neighbouring nations; and ask himself whether the circumstantial verifications of them are to be flippantly disposed of as illustrations of conjectures " extraordinarily felicitous."

Turn again to the predictions relating to the coming of Christ, which date from Paradise, and crowd the pages of the later prophets. With growing distinctness as the time of the Advent approached we find him described. He was to be of the seed of Abraham, of the tribe of Judah, of the house of David—was to be born of a virgin, in the town of Bethlehem. He was to combine the attributes of God and man. He was to be at once a King and a servant—a man of sorrows and the Prince of Peace. Are these predictions, which find such complete fulfilment in Jesus of Nazareth, to be explained as a series of fortunate conjectures? Or if, with some, we say that the prophecies concerning the Messiah are only expressions of the longings of the Hebrew people is it a matter of accident that they took a shape which

---

* Fairbairn on Prophecy, p. 206, American edition.

found such wonderful realization in the person of Jesus?

Surely, in attempting to eliminate the supernatural from Scripture men are obliged to resort to explanations which are far stranger than miracles, and in leaving the domain of faith they become the victims of credulity!

Equally unsuccessful, though in advance of the views just alluded to, is the hypothesis which accounts for the predictions of the Bible by attributing to the writers a very far-sighted sagacity. The advocates of this view refer us to the anticipations of scientific discovery in the Organon of Bacon, to the soul of Columbus "burdened with a material vision," to Wickliffe, Luther and Knox, who "in prophetic vision saw the great futurity of Protestantism which was to shake the foundation of the civilized world."*

Will any one pretend that these are analogous to the predictions of the Bible? There may be causes now at work the development of which in the proximate future we may predict with tolerable accuracy. The tendency of current events may in some instances be so obvious that we can safely form a judgment concerning the issue. But is

* Quoted by Fairbairn, Prophecy, p. 217

this equivalent to the utterance of prophecy concerning a remote future, and with reference to events which are not hinted at by anything in the present?

We may be safe in predicting in a general way great advance in scientific knowledge during the coming years. "That which men have done is but earnest of the things that they shall do." But what if the vision of the poet shall be realized, who

> "Saw the heavens filled with commerce, argosies of magic sails,
> Pilots of the purple twilight, dropping down with costly bales;
> Heard the heavens fill with shouting, and there rained a ghastly dew
> From the nations' airy navies grappling in the central blue."

Should we then number Tennyson among the prophets, and put these lines on a level with the predictions of Isaiah?

The prophecies of Scripture cannot be used as illustrations of political sagacity or scientific discernment. They do not consist of judgments concerning the issue of events in progress at the time of their utterance. They are distinct, discriminating, detailed predictions concerning events which could not have been suggested by anything which addressed itself to the observation of the keenest vision. Only an eye lit with heavenly brightness could see the shadow of the doom which was to overtake Tyre, "the crowning city, whose merchants were princes, and whose traffickers the honourable of the earth." Only when the divine hand had removed the veil which hid the future, could the prophet see the destruction which in coming years was to fall upon the proud, brazen-gated Babylon.

(4.) *Doctrines are taught in Scripture which must have come from God.*

We know that the doctrines of the Bible have God's sanction. For what is Hebrew history but a long lesson in monotheism? What were the bondage in Egypt, the wilderness journey, the Sinaitic legislation, the Babylonish captivity, but parts of an education designed to drill the Jews in the doctrine of God's unity and to teach them the meaning of true spiritual worship? What was the sacrificial system but a divine exposition of the doctrine of guilt? In like manner the doctrines peculiar to or more fully developed in the Christian system were, as we learn from Paul, matters of direct revelation. The trinity, the sacrifice of Christ, the work of the Spirit, justification by faith, the resurrection, the judgment, eternal retribution, were all inculcated, at least germinally, in the discourses of our Lord himself.

I wish, however, to draw attention to the fact that these doctrines not only *were*, but *must have been*, divinely revealed. They are stamped with the divine image and superscription. Their inherent excellence witnesses to their heavenly origin. The Bible representation of God is unique. Equally removed from the superstition which peopled hill and dale with deities, and the skepticisms which locked the universe in the arms of fate, it teaches of one ever-present, overruling Spirit. Excluding, on the one hand, the view which makes God only an exaggerated man and which clothes him in the imperfections of humanity, and on the other the Pantheism which strips him of his personality, it teaches us of a Person who is clothed in infinite perfections—whose attributes of holiness, of justice and of love are the prototypes of all that is noble in man, and in whose image man was created. It reveals to us a God at once a Sovereign and a Father; a God who satisfies our instincts of obligation and dependence; a God in whose nature blend the attributes of justice and of mercy—who manifests the one in his supreme regard for the majesty of law, while he exhibits the other in embarking the resources of Omnipotence in the work of man's redemption. The Bible conception of God, we may safely say, never could have originated in a human brain. The originality of Christ's character has been made use of, of late, as an argument for his divinity, and it is a strong one. A character which has won the admiration of the world, ideally perfect, though contrary to all antecedent ideals, cannot be a human invention. The same may be said of the code of Christian ethics. A system which commands the world's homage, though in open contradiction to the world's practice; which makes another's righteousness, not our merit, the ground of divine acceptance—self-sacrifice, not selfishness, the rule of Christian living; which prescribes love rather than hate, forgiveness rather than resentment, endurance rather than revenge; which tells us that humility is better than ambition, philanthropy than conquest,—a system at once so grand and so far beyond the compass of heathen thought, must have come from God. The Christian system meets the wants of the race, and this corroborates its claim to be a divine revelation. The Bible brings to light the deep things and the secret things of man's spiritual nature. It is the interpreter of the conscience. It expounds man's sense of guilt, and throws light upon the instinct which prompts him to pray and offer sacrifice. It explains his dissatisfaction with all that is earthly by widening the field of his vision and disclosing the glories of a better land. And while it affirms the judgments of the conscience concerning his sin and destiny, it also gives him solid ground for his hopes by assuring him that the blood of Jesus has been spilled in expiation of his guilt, and that the love of the tripersonal God has been enlisted for his recovery.

Nor does the mysteriousness of some of the doctrines at all shake our faith in their divinity; it rather strengthens it; for it may be taken for granted that what has originated in a human mind is not beyond human comprehension. By dint of persevering study, men are able to get to the bottom of what Plato or Shakespeare has said, but no human mind can fathom the depths or explore the secrets of the Bible doctrines of the Trinity and the Incarnation. The fact that the learning and industry of nineteen Christian centuries have been expended on the investigation of these doctrines without exhausting their meaning or divesting them of mystery, is very good reason for our believing them to be divine. Nay, the very doctrines which are sometimes used as arguments against the Bible may be fairly employed in its defence, and in *the fact that they conflict with each other* we may find a confirmation of their claims. Predestination and free agency are alike taught in the Bible. They pervade the sacred volume. They are both emphasized. They are both insisted on by the same writers. They follow hard upon each other in the same chapter. And yet no human mind can reduce them to unity. It is easy to construct a consistent system on either doctrine alone, and systems of this one-sided kind have been built. We may build on God's sovereignty as a foundation, and fatalism is the result. We may build on man's freedom as a foundation, and Pelagianism is the result. The Bible system, however, is that which recognizes both truths, and concedes their irreconcilability because they transcend human comprehension. But is it supposable that a system which incorporates two elements so obviously incompatible, so far as our reason is concerned, could have originated with man? Would doctrines which have tasked the faith of Christians in all ages ever have suggested themselves to a human speculator as true? Would a writer of Paul's learning and penetration have failed to see that these two ideas, which he insists upon in his Epistles, are, to all human appearance, in open conflict? And could he ever have persuaded himself that they were true, or have spoken so confidently concerning them, if his faith had not rested on the authority of divine revelation? To the candid mind there can be but one answer to these questions. Divine authority alone could have overcome the protest which reason would have raised against the apparent discrepancy of these doctrines. We can account for their existence in Scripture only on the supposition that they came from God, and that the discrepancies disappear in a unity which is above us and out of sight.

We shall learn by further inquiry whether the Bible gives us a human version of divine revelations, or whether the record itself is a divine production. In the mean time, let us mark the progress we have made in this chapter by adopting the formula of a theory of partial inspiration;—* The Bible *contains* the Word of God.

* The distinction between the Bible and the Word of God was first brought into prominence by Töllner, about the middle of last century. See Hagenbach, Hist. Doctrine, American edition, vol. ii. p. 466.

CHAPTER III.

THE WHOLE BIBLE IS GOD'S MESSAGE.

WE were led in our last chapter to a very important conclusion. A survey of Scripture teaches us that our religion is throughout a revelation from God. The object of our faith is God manifest in the flesh. The doctrines which constitute our creed came from God, and are attested by the most marked manifestations of the divine presence and power; so that the Christian has a right to feel the most unshaken confidence in his religion. This conclusion will now aid us in establishing the authoritative character of the Scriptures. The next question of an inquirer would be, "Does the Bible contain the *authoritative* and, so to speak, the *official* account of God's revelation?" The question does not imply that any suspicion exists with regard to the truthfulness of the account. We have reached the position which makes any such suspicion impossible, not to say illogical. But a true account is one thing, and an official another. Macaulay's history is true, but it is different from the State papers from which he derived his information. The question I have raised has a very important bearing on the subject of inspiration. For if it can be shown that the Bible was meant to be the authoritative account of a plan of salvation, the very strongest presumption will be afforded for its infallibility. Did God intend, we may suppose an inquirer to ask, that the accounts of the miracles, divine utterances, prophecies, doctrines which we find in the Scripture should be put on record for the use of coming generations, and do the records which we have carry his sanction? Do we know that the writers of Scripture were authorized to write the books of the canon? The official rank of most of the writers is enough to give the weight of authority to what they wrote. Moses was the accredited leader of God's people; he wrought miracles in proof of his divine commission; enjoyed face to face interviews with Deity; received oral instructions concerning the institutions embodied in his history. Do we need proof that Moses' writings had the divine sanction, when his whole public life brought him into official relations with God? When the prophets uttered their messages under divine inspiration, it can hardly be said that their prophecies were less authoritative because put into a written form. They did not lose their divine sanction by being put on record. Nor is it necessary for us to have evidence for the authoritative character of the apostolic writings beyond the commission given to the apostles to preach, teach, organize the Church and administer its affairs. The divine sanction which adhered to their preaching and administration may be fairly taken as *primâ facie* evidence in behalf of the authority of their writings.

Let us look after the question in another light. The great idea of the Bible is redemption. Everything in Scripture crystallizes round the person of Christ. The burden of the volume is salvation by faith. A gospel for the world, a gospel for all time, a gospel whose benefits to be enjoyed must be known—this is the teaching of Scripture. It reveals a gospel which contemplates propagation. The *telling* of it is not an accident, and therefore a matter unprovided for. It exists to be told. It was given to be preached. The inference is natural, therefore, that the gospel to be world-wide must be written.

The case stands thus. The Bible either contains

an authoritative account of the Gospel, or we have a religion divinely revealed, with no divine care for its preservation—a religion meant to be universal with no provision for its perpetuation. We must receive the Bible as containing an official account of God's will, or express our obligation to the writers of Scripture for the literary impulse which prompted them to put on record the facts on the preservation of which the hopes of the world depended.

To my mind one of the best evidences that the Bible is a revelation *from* God is that it is a revelation *of* God.

Further. The doctrine of the Incarnation, as has been already intimated, unifies the Bible. The sacrifice of Christ is the key to the Jewish ritual. The advent of the Messiah is the fulfilment of prophecy. The Bible without Christ is a riddle; the Bible interpreted with Calvary in view is the unfolding of a single plan. Throughout the volume the same "increasing purpose runs." The conviction grows upon the mind, with increased study of the Scriptures, that they were meant to exhibit the progressive development of a scheme of grace which culminated in the gift of Jesus and the offer of salvation to all who bel'eve in his name. And this question addresses itself to our judgment, Is it possible that writers who were separated by the lapse of centuries, and who were actuated only by the ordinary motives which prompt to literary composition, could have produced a series of books which would constitute the complete and congruous system of truth which we find in the Bible?

But it may be said that some of the historical portions of the Bible contain information which was within easy reach of an ordinary historian. The books of Kings and Chronicles and the Acts of the Apostles, for instance, might easily have been written by men who had access to the ordinary avenues of knowledge. It would be anticipating what I shall have to say when I speak more particularly of the proofs of plenary inspiration, to deny this assertion here. I shall admit the propriety of the question which is based on it, How do we know that these historical events of Scripture were intended to form part of a divine message? And the answer is, Because of the relations in which they stand to other portions of Scripture.

It is a peculiarity of the Christian religion that history is made the channel of communicating supernatural truth. The doctrines all have an historical setting. Prophecy and history are so correlated that they illustrate and confirm each other. The historical portions of the Bible are written with such evident reference to the illustration of a single scheme, are so plainly subordinate to and in harmony with the great idea of Redemption, that we should be warranted in placing them on a level with the strictly prophetic or doctrinal books, though direct Scripture testimony on the point were wanting. It is impossible that authors, acting without concert, on their individual responsibility, could have produced a series of writings so wonderfully corroborative of those portions of Scripture which are avowedly the records of divine communications.

But the Scriptures themselves are far from being silent on the question before us. They intimate very clearly that all the parts of the Bible stand on the same level in point of authority, and together constitute a divine message. There are passages which intimate that portions of Scripture at least were written by direct command. Thus, concerning the discomfiture of Amalek, we read, "And the Lord said unto Moses, Write this for a memorial in a book and rehearse it in the ears of Joshua." Ex. xvii. 14. So in Numbers xxxiii. 1, 2: "These are the journeys of the children of Israel which went forth out of the land of Egypt with the armies under the hand of Moses and Aaron. And Moses wrote their going out according to their journeys, by commandment of the Lord." Ex. xxiv. 4: "And Moses wrote all the words of the Lord. . . . . . And he took the book of the covenant and read in the audience of the people, and they said, All that the Lord hath said will we do and be obedient." Ex. xxxiv. 27: "And the Lord said unto Moses, Write thou these words, for after the tenor of these words have I made a covenant with thee and with Israel."

We read likewise that Jeremiah was commanded to take a roll and write in it the words which God had spoken to him against Judah and Jerusalem. Habakkuk was charged to write the vision and make it plain. The writer of the Apocalypse distinctly states that he wrote his visions by divine command.

Daniel and Zechariah both testify that in their day there was a collection of sacred writings which had claims upon the faith of the people and were clothed with divine sanctions. Dan. ix. 2: "And I Daniel understood by the books the number of the years when the word of the Lord came to Jeremiah the prophet that he would accomplish seventy years in the desolations of Jerusalem." Zech. vii. 7: "Should ye not hear the words which the Lord hath cried by the former prophets when Jerusalem was inhabited and in prosperity, and the cities thereof round about her, when men inhabited the south and the plain?" Verse 12: "Yea, they made their hearts as an adamant stone lest they should hear the law, and the words which the Lord of hosts hath sent in his Spirit by the former prophets."

The Pentateuch is spoken of repeatedly in the Bible as God's law. Ps. xix. 7: "The law of the Lord is perfect." Ps. cxix. 1: "Blessed are the undefiled in the way who walk in the law of the Lord." Neh. viii. 8: "So they read in the book in the law of God distinctly, and gave the sense, and caused them to understand the reading." Verse 14: "And they found written in the law which the Lord had commanded by Moses" (see Lev. xxiii. 34, 42) "that the children of Israel should dwell in booths in the feast of the seventh month." Luke ii. 23: "As it is written in the law of the Lord" (see Ex. xiii. 2), "Every male that openeth the womb shall be called holy unto the Lord."

It is a sufficient reason for holding all the books of the Old Testament in equal reverence, that they all had a place in the Canon, and were held sacred by the Jewish nation. They were all included among the "oracles of God," of which the Jews were made the guardians. Rom. iii. 1, 2. And more than this, the Old Testament was recognized by our Saviour himself, and quoted as authoritative by him and his apostles. They accepted the Jewish Scriptures as God's message, and made no distinctions of rank between the several books. Under the name Scripture they embraced everything between Genesis and Malachi. "Think not, said Jesus, that I am come to destroy the law or the prophets: I am not come to destroy, but to fulfill." Paul gives decided though incidental testimony to the authority of the historical books in Rom. xi. 2, where, quoting from 1 Kings xix. 14, he says, "Wot ye not what the *Scripture* saith of Elias, how he maketh intercession to God against Israel?" etc.

There are many other passages besides these which have been adduced in which the Scriptures assert their authoritative character. Thus our Saviour said, "Search the Scriptures, for in them ye think ye have eternal life, and they are they which testify of me." John v. 39. "Had ye believed Moses, ye would have believed me: for he wrote of me. But if ye believe not his writings, how shall ye believe my words?" John v. 46. "If they hear not Moses and the prophets, neither would they be persuaded, though one rose from the dead." Luke xvi. 31. He reproves the two disciples on the way to Emmaus because they lacked faith in the Scriptures: "O fools, and slow of heart, to believe all that the prophets have spoken." Luke xxiv. 25.

Peter exhorted those to whom his epistle was addressed to be "mindful of the words which had been spoken before by the holy prophets." Paul commends Timothy for his knowledge of the holy Scriptures, which were able to make him wise unto salvation, and which are profitable for doctrine, for reproof, for correction, for instruction in righteousness, that the man of God may be perfect, thoroughly furnished unto all good works. 2 Tim. iii. 15–17.

The same apostle says to the Christians at Rome, "Whatsoever things were written aforetime, were written for our learning, that we through patience and comfort of the Scriptures might have hope." Rom xv. 4. A passage in the Second Epistle of Peter iii. 15–16, while teaching that the Scriptures are authoritative, and that it is dangerous to pervert them, gives very explicit testimony to the equality of the New Testament with the Old: "Even as our beloved brother Paul also according to the wisdom given unto him hath written unto you, as also in all his epistles speaking in them of these things; in which are some things hard to be understood, which they that are unlearned and unstable wrest, as they do also the *other Scriptures*, to their own destruction."

Citations like these might be multiplied, but these are enough for our purpose. Let us notice their bearing on the argument. The object of the writers in penning these passages was not to *establish* the divine authority of the Old Testament. These passages are incidental allusions to a well-established fact. When Ezra mentions the book of the Law; when Matthew refers to the law of the Lord; when the Saviour refers to Moses and the prophets; when the apostles, all through their writings, show their reverence for the Old Testament by prefacing their quotations with the words, What saith the Scripture, The Scripture saith, It is written, etc., they were uttering no strange sentiments, were broaching no new doctrines. Hence these casual references to the authority of the Old Testament are the strongest testimony we can have, because they show that it had such a place in the minds of those to whom the New Testament writers addressed themselves, that argument was unnecessary.

It is proper, moreover, to remember that the authoritative character of the Bible does not rest exclusively on specific Scripture proofs. That the Scriptures were meant as a divine message is sufficiently indicated in the fact that they contain a revelation of supernatural truth, and together constitute an organic unity. So that these texts, even if they should seem inadequate to establish the proposition which I have placed at the beginning of this chapter, are conclusive when considered as corroborative of a proposition which rests on other ground as well.

CHAPTER IV.

DIVINE AGENCY EMPLOYED IN THE COMPOSITION OF SCRIPTURE.

WE reach solid ground when we are assured that the Bible is the authoritative expression of God's will. But we cannot stop at this point in our investigation. We naturally desire to know how the books of Scripture were produced.

The fact that the Bible is a divine message does not necessarily imply that it is a divine writing. The supernatural character of its contents does not settle the question concerning the agency employed in its composition. Our inquiries have as yet taught us nothing on the subject of inspiration. God might have allowed the prophets to record the revelations made to them, without exerting any further influence on them. Through the ordinary exercise of memory they might have preserved, with a degree of accuracy, the substance of the supernatural communications. For aught we have learned yet, the historical portions of the Bible may have been composed under the general superintendence of God, without any special exercise of divine agency in the choice of words or in the arrangement of materials. And if we were without evidence that the sacred writers received divine assistance in the composition of Scripture, we could not deny the claims of the Bible to be a divine message. We could not assert its infallibility, to be sure; we could not say that the message had undergone no change in passing through a human medium; but it would nevertheless possess sufficient accuracy to render him inexcusable who should refuse to take it as the guide of his life.

Is the Bible a human or a divine account of supernatural revelations? Does God speak to us in his own words, or do the sacred writers give us their version of what they have seen and heard? Does the divine message come to us as the direct utterance of God's mind, or has it taken the colouring of human imperfections in passing through the channel of human authorship? Now, the fact that the Bible is God's message raises the strongest presumption in favour of its infallibility. God speaks to men through the written word. This is the only avenue by which man can expect divine communications to come. This volume was meant to be a complete and perpetual embodiment of God's will in the matter of human salvation. It is fair for us to suppose that God would preserve it from errors incident to mere human authorship? We surely have every reason to expect that God would not give the world a book which makes known the only way of escape from divine wrath without guarding it against inaccuracies in the statement of facts and mistakes in the exposition of doctrine. We may fairly presume that God would not give us his revelations at second hand, but that he would place on the documents which contain it the stamp of divine authorship.

This presumption is confirmed by several considerations, aside altogether from the texts which explicitly teach the inspiration of the Scriptures.

(1.) *Extended accounts of divine communications.*

It has been already said that the writers of Scripture might have reported the *substance* of the communications addressed to them, without supernatural aid. We must remember, however, that in many instances the Scriptures purport to give us not the substance, but a *verbatim* report, of what God said. Let the reader turn, for example, to Exodus xxv.-xxx. These chapters contain the oral instructions addressed to Moses concerning the setting up of the tabernacle. They are so varied, so novel, so disconnected, so minute, that the most retentive memory, we may say without hesitation, could not safely be entrusted with them. And yet, fidelity in the mention of the smallest details was necessary to the carrying out of God's will. The most trifling thing—the fringe of a curtain, the colour of a vestment, the knop of a candlestick—if it was of sufficient importance to be a matter of divine instruction, was important enough to be correctly recorded. The best explanation of Moses' fidelity is, that God kept him from error by aiding in the composition of his books.

(2.) *Marvellous accuracy of Scripture.*

The accuracy of the sacred writers goes far beyond that of other historians. The Bible is accurate to a superhuman extent. It is not only wanting in mistakes sufficient to invalidate its claims to veracity, but it is not chargeable with *any* mistakes. It not only defies the industry of those who hunt through its pages for errors enough to overthrow the doctrine of plenary inspiration, but these errors are missing to such a degree as to leave a very strong conviction on the mind that human agency was not left alone in its composition.

We should not be surprised to find that writers

who lacked the training necessary for the work of the historian should allow errors, in regard to matters incidental to their main design, to creep into their writings. The four evangelists may have given us a faithful account of the events in our Lord's life of which they were eye-witnesses, even though their books were open to criticism in the passages which allude to a complex political system. But the most searching criticism brings to light no error in their pages. And this is the more remarkable, inasmuch as the Gospels and Acts of the Apostles cover a period in the history of Palestine which is marked by sudden and frequent political changes. Within half a century this little strip of country was "a single united kingdom under a native ruler; a set of principalities under native ethnarchs and tetrarchs; a country in part containing such principalities, in part reduced to the condition of a Roman province; a kingdom reunited once more under a native sovereign, and a country reduced wholly under Rome and governed by procurators dependent on the president of Syria, but still subject, in certain respects, to the Jewish monarch of a neighbouring territory." How do we explain the fact that four writers, who, we may suppose, had not had the experience which would fit them for close attention to the details of government, were able to thread their way with discriminating accuracy through the confusing system of mixed Roman and Jewish politics? Perhaps it would be too much to say that Luke could not have obtained without supernatural aid the minute information which he has embodied in the Acts of the Apostles. But it will certainly appear strange to any one who will consider it, that the companion of the Apostle Paul, visiting the different cities of the Mediterranean for the purpose rather of introducing a new religion than of gathering information, should show such minute acquaintance with the details of Roman government and jurisprudence, and should be able to refer without mistake to local customs and make use of words of only local currency. An ordinary writer, to whose main design these matters were purely incidental, would not have been particular to tell us that Sergius Paulus was a proconsul (ἀνθύπατος, translated *deputy* in our version), or that the rulers of Thessalonica were called *politarchs*, or that Philippi was a colony, or that the most prominent man in Ephesus was called townclerk (γραμματεύς), or that the word which the Ephesians used to signify *a worshipper* means literally a *temple-sweeper* (νεωκόρον). Nor would it be

DIVINE AGENCY IN THEIR COMPOSITION. 59

possible, without special labour, to avoid confusion, if he should attempt, in casual references to the political status of different cities or to their officials, to make use of technical phrases. Yet Luke makes no mistake, never misapplies his epithets and never takes shelter under general terms. We should hardly have supposed that the author of the book of Acts had acquired such minute acquaintance with nautical terms and nautical affairs that he could give a detailed account of Paul's perilous voyage from Jerusalem to Rome. Yet this account has been laboriously examined and carefully compared with known facts of the present day by persons professionally conversant with nautical matters. The result has been, not only to establish the veritable and trustworthy character of the narrative, but to enable the whole voyage to be traced as accurately as if a log-book of the particulars had been handed down from that day to this.*

And let it be remembered that this minute accuracy extends to the whole Bible. There is certainly a very decided indication that supernatural agency was employed in the composition of the Scriptures, in the fact that a volume comprising sixty different compositions, bridging a period of

* Garbett, God's Word Written, p. 233.

four thousand years, containing revelations of the past and predictions of the future, embodying the annals of a nation and the religious experience of individuals, setting forth a system of doctrine for all men and every age, and yet full of allusions to matters of mere local interest, is absolutely free from error. We are aware that exception might be taken to this unqualified statement concerning the accuracy of Scripture; but it is true, nevertheless, that the appliances of the most exact modern scholarship have been brought to bear upon the study of the Bible, and that, with the exception of a few cases of contradiction, clearly attributable to the fault of copyists, the deniers of inspiration have not been able to prove against the Scriptures the charge of falsehood.

(3.) *Motives ascribed to men, and reasons assigned for divine acts.*

The sacred writers speak as assuredly concerning the motives of men as if they had gained admittance into the chambers of the soul, and learned the secrets which are known only to the Searcher of hearts. They even go so far as to tell us how human actions appear in God's sight, and give us circumstantial interpretations of the providential dealings of the Most High. We can explain this peculiar feature in the sacred histories only by the supposition that the authors of them were aided by the omniscient One.

We read, Exodus xiv. 5, "And it was told the king of Egypt that the people fled; and the heart of Pharaoh and of his servants was turned against the people, and they said, Why have we done this, that we have let Israel go from serving us?" etc. How did Moses know how Pharaoh felt or what he said when he heard of Israel's escape?

Again, 1 Chron. v. 26: "And the God of Israel stirred up the spirit of Pul king of Assyria, and the spirit of Tilgath-pilneser king of Assyria, and he carried them away," etc.

2 Chron. xxviii. 5: "Wherefore the Lord his God delivered him into the hand of the king of Syria," etc. Verse 19: "For the Lord brought Judah low, because of Ahaz king of Israel," etc. 2 Chron. xxxvi. 15: "And the Lord God of their fathers sent to them by his messengers, rising up betimes and sending; because he had compassion on his people and on his dwelling-place." Verse 17: "Therefore he brought upon them the king of the Chaldees, who slew their young men with the sword," etc.

What would we think of the historian who

should presume to state the reasons which swayed the divine mind with reference to national history? "Who hath known the mind of the Lord, and who hath been his counsellor?"

1 Chron. x. 13: "So Saul died for his transgression which he committed against the Lord," etc.

1 Chron. xxi. 1: "And Satan stood up against Israel, and provoked David to number Israel."

How did the sacred writer get the information which he has given us in these verses?

Matt. ix. 21: "For she said within herself, If I may but touch his garment I shall be whole."

Verse 36: "But when he saw the multitude he was moved with compassion on them because they fainted," etc.

Could human insight discern the thoughts which entered the mind of the woman when she touched the hem of the Saviour's garment, or understand the feelings of Jesus when he looked upon the multitude?

If these passages had been cited at an earlier stage in our investigation, it might have been said that they expressed only the *surmises* of the sacred writers. But we must remember that the writers of Scripture were divinely commissioned to write the books of the canon, and that the Bible is an authoritative expression of God's will. We cannot suppose therefore that the authors of Scripture could have made the serious assertions which we have quoted, and allowed them to stand on their pages as matters of history, if they had been fictions of their own brain. The statements would not have been made if the writers had not known them to be true, and they could not have known them to be true unless they had received information from God.

Notice now that these quotations do not belong to the class of passages which are avowedly the record of divine communications. The writers do not tell us that God said that Satan tempted David to number Israel, or that Saul died because he asked counsel of one who had a familiar spirit. They make these statements in the same way that they narrate the most ordinary facts. On the supposition that the whole record was shaped under divine superintendence, and that the divine mind aided the writers in the performance of their task, it is easy to understand why the passages we have quoted and many similar ones should have been accompanied by no special reference to divine revelation. But if the sacred writers, though acting under divine commission, were, notwithstanding, the sole authors of the books they wrote, it is strange that when they made statements which they could not or ought not to have made unless they received divine revelations, they did not substantiate their accounts by giving their authority.

Of course it does not follow that because these and similar passages must have been written at the suggestion of God or by his assistance, therefore the whole Bible was so written. They are, however, in a measure, confirmatory of a very strong presumption in favour of the infallibility of the Scriptures; and the argument based upon them, though not demonstrative, is a link in the chain of evidence by which the conviction is produced that the writers of Scripture were aided in the work entrusted to them by contact with the divine mind.

(4.) *Reticence of the writers, and their wisdom in the selection of facts.*

We have already seen that the sacred writers were divinely commissioned. We may suppose, moreover, that ample resources were at their command for the performance of their work. We may grant that, possibly, Moses had access to pre-existing documents in writing the history of the antediluvian world. But this will not explain the principle by which the writers were governed in the selection of facts. We cannot suppose that each writer had such latitude of discretion that he was allowed to put on record just what he supposed relevant to the purpose the Scriptures were designed to serve. The unity which pervades the Bible forbids the idea. The Bible was written with reference to a plan. Its parts fit into each other like the pieces of a mosaic. The writers have selected with consummate wisdom the salient points in the spiritual history of man. They dispose in a few sentences of topics on which ordinary writers love to dilate, and weave their materials into the form best adapted for the exhibition of a progressive plan of divine grace. For the accomplishment of this task they needed, it seems to me, the constant guidance of divine wisdom.

It is a noticeable feature in the Scriptures that the writers often omit the mention of details in matters concerning which we are naturally curious, and avoid the display of any personal feeling on occasions which would naturally elicit it.

For illustration we may refer to the evangelists. How natural it would have been for them, had they been ordinary biographers, to have given us more information concerning the early years of the Saviour. John, especially, whose house furnished a home to the bereaved mother of our Lord, we would think, was in possession of ample materials for this work. How can we better explain this reticence than by supposing that the evangelists acted under divine instructions? Again, how wonderfully brief and unimpassioned is the language of the evangelists in the several accounts of our Lord's death! They all record the circumstances of the crucifixion, but not a syllable breathing indignation against the enemies of the Saviour is to be found in their pages. How strange it is that the intimate companions of Jesus should write his life without giving expression to a word of eulogy, and record his cruel death without entering a protest against the sin of crucifying the Lord of glory!

(5.) *Relations subsisting between the several books of the New Testament.*

The argument from design has been already used to show that the several books of the Bible stand on the same level, and that their authors held a divine commission to write the Scriptures. We cannot help thinking that it goes farther—that it testifies to a direct divine influence exerted upon the writers in the composition of the Bible. Let us illustrate the force of the argument by reference to the relations which the several books of the New Testament sustain to each other.

The New Testament opens with a fourfold biography of Christ. It was right that we should grow familiar with his life before we were taught the doctrinal import of his work—right that we should know the facts on which the doctrines are based before our attention was called to elaborate expositions of the doctrines themselves.

The four evangelists sustain a definite relation to each other, and together give us a complete portraiture of the Saviour. The three synoptic gospels bring into greater prominence the human side of Christ's nature; while the gospel according to John brings out with greater distinctness the divine side, and opens with the sublime announcement, "In the beginning was the Word, and the Word was with God, and the Word was God." Again, Matthew's gospel was evidently written for the Jew. His object is to show the relation of Christ to the theocracy as the Fulfiller of law and prophecy. Luke's gospel was meant for the Gentile; he accordingly represents Christ not as related to Judaism, but to the race. While Matthew's genealogy shows that Christ is the son of Abraham, Luke's represents him as a descendant of Adam, and therefore the brother of the whole human family.

From the life of Jesus we turn to the history of the society of which he was the founder. The first history of the Christian Church was written by Luke, and we read it in the Acts of the Apostles. The theme of apostolic preaching was Christ— Christ crucified, Christ risen. The former was the fact of greatest doctrinal importance—the latter was the fact of greatest evidential importance. With these two facts in their possession they were not afraid to preach even in Jerusalem the gospel of reconciliation.

We are enabled in the book of Acts to watch the first steps in the progress of the infant Church. The gospel was preached first to the Jews, then to the Samaritans, then to Cornelius by Peter, and then to the world at large by the great apostle of the Gentiles. By degrees the channel of divine grace widened; by degrees, as Providence opened the way, the glad tidings spread; by degrees the purpose of God to include the Gentiles in the embrace of the gospel disclosed itself to those who were privileged to be its first preachers.

But after the Jew had professed faith in Christ, after the Gentile had cast away his idols and numbered himself among the followers of Jesus—what then? Was the work complete? Far from it. A great change was to be effected in the character of the convert. New affections were to be implanted—new direction given to the energies—higher views of life were to be instilled—more definite ideas of doctrine to be imparted—old habits were to be relinquished, old forms of thought to be abandoned. Having enlisted in Christ's service, he was to be drilled; having taken his place in Christ's school, he was to be instructed. The foundation of a holy life being laid, he must be edified; being justified, he was to be sanctified. Accordingly, the succeeding books of the New Testament assume the epistolatory form. We have a collection of letters addressed to those who are already in the Church—within the pale of Christian brotherhood—"to the saints and faithful brethren in Christ Jesus." And in these letters we have a picture of early Christian piety; we have an opportunity of observing the influence of the gospel upon those who have but recently embraced it; we become acquainted with the trials through which the converts from heathenism passed, and the temptations to which they were exposed. These letters are full of Christian sympathy, are replete with principles for the guidance of Christian life, and are largely occupied with expansions of Christian doctrine and exhortations to holy living.

And, what is more, they sustain a definite relation to each other, We have the Epistle to the Romans devoted to the settlement of the question prompted by the universal conscience, " How shall man be just with God ?" The Epistles to the Corinthians, practical in their aim, with an exposition of the great law of Christian expediency, and written in opposition to the pride of Greek philosophy and the licentiousness of a Grecian city; and these are followed by the Epistle to the Galatians, designed to strip the fetters of legalism from those whom Christ declared to be free. Each fills an important place. Each contributes to the full unfolding of the plan of salvation—All together make one symmetrical organism, one consistent body of truth. No trace of disagreement is to be found in the doctrines of the Epistles. They present the truth in different phases, but it is the same truth. Though Peter was the subject of Paul's reproof, we discover no divergence in his Epistles from the doctrines taught by the great apostle. "The faith expounded by Paul kindles into fervent hope in the words of Peter, and expands into sublime love in those of John." *

Can we believe that the New Testament has assumed its present form by accident? Is it possible that a collection of writings exhibiting a progressive development of Christian truth, and closing with a prophecy concerning the future glory of the Church, could have been produced by a number of writers acting without concert, unless they acted under divine influence?

* Bernard, Progress of Doctrine in New Testament.

For the ideas embodied in the above remarks on the relations of the several books of the New Testament to each other, the writer is indebted to the admirable volume of the Bampton Lectures.

CHAPTER V.

PLENARY INSPIRATION.

THERE is still room for inquiry concerning the *extent* to which divine agency was employed in the composition of Scripture. Were *all* the books of the Bible written under supernatural influence?— Canticles as well as the Pentateuch, Esther as well as the Acts? Do we know whether the divine mind operated on the writers in composing everything which they had put on record? Was the agency which God exercised in the structure of the Bible akin to that of an architect in the erection of an edifice? Did he only superintend the work, suggesting to the sacred writers what facts to embody in the records, and giving the plan according to which the materials were to be shaped? Did the human authors of Scripture exercise their unassisted faculties in composing the books of the Canon, save when divine revelation was needed to supplement the narrowness of human knowledge, and divine wisdom to correct the imperfections of human judgment? Or did God exercise such an influence on the minds of the sacred writers that *every part of the Bible* is a product of the divine mind? Did he suggest the *thoughts* which have been put on record, and leave the writers to the exercise of their own discretion in the choice of *words*, or are the words of Scripture the words of God? In short, Have God and man divided the labour of composing the Bible, and do they therefore share the honour, or is the Bible God's book from beginning to end? These questions all resolve themselves into the one which I shall endeavour to answer in this chapter: Do the Scriptures teach the doctrine of Partial or Plenary Inspiration? There is ample material for a reply to this inquiry, at least so far as the Old Testament is concerned, as the following considerations will show:

(1.) *Names applied to the Old Testament by writers of the New.*

The Old Testament is referred to upward of fifty times in the New Testament as *the Scripture* or *the Scriptures.* In Romans i. 2, it is called the Holy Scriptures (γραφαῖς ἁγίαις); in 2 Tim. iii. 15 the Hallowed Writings (ἱερὰ γράμματα); in Rom. iii. 2, Heb. v. 12, 1 Pet. iv. 11, The Oracles of God (τὰ λόγια τοῦ Θεοῦ).

The word γραφη, Scripture, it is true, may be applied as well to one kind of writing as another. But the point to be noticed is, that it is employed in the New Testament in a restricted sense. It is always used to designate the Old Testament, together with portions of the New. Hence, though applicable to every species of composition, it has in New Testament usage the force of a proper name, just as our word BIBLE has. When the evangelist spake of *the Scriptures,* there was no danger of their being misunderstood. There was no necessity for asking, What Scriptures? any more than there is any doubt what work we refer to when we speak of *the Book* or *the Bible.* It is clear, therefore, that the Old Testament held such a place in the minds of the apostles and of the whole Hebrew people that it was considered as *the writings par excellence.* And further, the application of a common name to the whole Old Testament places all the books on the same level. If one book ranks as a divine writing, we cannot give a lower place to another. If some of the books were divine writings and others only human compositions, we should expect to find the distinction indicated in some way. But nothing of the kind is hinted at in the New Testament. The whole Hebrew Bible is included under the epithets, Holy Scripture, the Hallowed Writings, the Oracles of God.

(2.) *Deference paid to the Old Testament.*

The references to the Old Testament which we find in the Gospels, the Acts and the Epistles prove that their writers regarded it not only as an authority, but as an infallible authority; not only as a record of divine communications, but as one unmixed with human error. They appeal with perfect confidence to the Old Testament, and plainly tell us that the Scripture must be fulfilled. They do this, moreover, without any protest on the part of the Jewish nation. However much the Jews rejected the reasonings which the apostles based on the Old Testament, we have no hint that they ever denied the infallibility of the oracles of which they were made the guardians. Passages are quoted from the Old Testament as predictions verified in New Testament history, the relevancy of which depends upon the assumption that they are a correct—a verbally correct—report of divine communications. We may illustrate this by reference to the Gospel according to Matthew: "When he arose he took the young child and his mother by night and departed into Egypt and was there till the death of Herod, that it might be fulfilled which was spoken of the Lord by the prophet, saying, Out of Egypt have I called my son." Matt. ii. 14, 15: see Hosea xi. 1. " He departed into Galilee, and leaving Nazareth, he came and dwelt in Capernaum, which is upon the sea-coast in the borders of Zabulon and Nephthalim, that it might be fulfilled which was spoken by Esaias the prophet, saying, The land of Zabulon and the land of Nephthalim by the way of the sea beyond Jordan, Galilee of the Gentiles; the people which sat in darkness saw a great light, and to them which sat in the region and shadow of death light is sprung up." Matt. iv. 12; see Isa. ix. 1. " Then sent Jesus two disciples, saying unto them, Go into the village over against you, and straightway ye shall find an ass tied and a colt with her; loose them and bring them unto me. . . . . All this was done that the Scripture might be fulfilled which was spoken by the prophet, saying, Tell ye the daughter of Zion, Behold thy King cometh unto thee, meek, and sitting on an ass, and a colt the foal of an ass." Matt. xxi. 1, 5; see Zech. ix. 9. "These parted his garments, casting lots, that it might be fulfilled which was spoken by the prophet, They parted my garments among them, and upon my vesture did they cast lots." Matt. xxvii. 35; Ps. xxii. 18.

The confidence with which the evangelist makes these citations is a proof that the infallibility of the Old Testament was a settled point in the mind of the writer and in the minds of his Hebrew readers. For it is clear that if error is anywhere incorporated in the Old Testament, only revelation can bring it to light. If the writers of Scripture have mixed their own sentiments with the divine communications, it is not in the power of human discernment to separate one from the other. It would be impossible, therefore, in that case, to speak positively of any particular verse or clause of a verse and say that it is the word of God. Unless the Old Testament is an infallible expression of God's mind, the language of the evangelist is open to very serious criticism, and room is afforded for the charge that Matthew has based very weighty inferences on very insufficient testimony. For the question very naturally arises, How do we know whether the passages which have been cited are not human utterances, which have been inadvertently incorporated in the divine message? If error is present anywhere in the Old Testament, why may not these very citations be open to this objection? Nor does it relieve the difficulty to say that the authority of the passages quoted by the evangelist is indicated by the fact that Matthew was divinely commissioned to write his gospel, and must therefore have been in a position to speak positively regarding these citations. This does not alter the fact that Matthew appealed to these passages on the simple ground that they are contained in the Old Testament. The force of his citations consists in the fact that in addressing Jewish readers he appealed to an authority whose infallibility they were prepared to admit. They had no supernatural means of discriminating truth from error, and therefore, unless they were ready to concede that *everything* in the Old Testament carried the divine sanction, it could not be expected that they should see any propriety in the assertions that the leading events in the life of Christ were shaped so as to bring about the fulfilment of some incidental expressions scattered through the writings of the prophets. The phrase, "*that it might be fulfilled,*" which occurs so often in the gospels, proves that the evangelists and those to whom they addressed themselves shared a common belief in the infallibility of the Old Testament.

(3.) *This infallibility asserted by the Saviour.*

Jesus gave very explicit testimony on this point. It will be sufficient to quote the passages which contain it. "And Jesus answered and said unto them, are ye come as against a thief with swords and with staves to take me? I was daily with you in the temple, teaching and ye took me not; *but the Scripture must be fulfilled.*" Mark xiv. 49. "Jesus answered and said unto them, Ye do err, not knowing the Scriptures nor the power of God." Matt. xxii. 29. "And he (Jesus) said unto them, O fools and slow of heart to believe all that the prophets have spoken! Ought not Christ to have suffered these things, and to enter into his glory? And beginning at Moses and all the prophets, he expounded unto them in all these Scriptures the things concerning himself." Luke xxiv. 25–27.

"And he said, These are the words which I spake unto you while I was yet with you, that *all things must be fulfilled which were written in the law of Moses, and in the prophets and in the Psalms concerning me.* Then opened he their understanding that they might understand the Scriptures, and said unto them, Thus it is written, and thus it behooved Christ to suffer," etc. Luke xxiv. 44–46.

"Think not that I am come to destroy the law or the prophets; I am not come to destroy, but to fulfil, for verily, I say unto you, Till heaven and earth pass, *one jot or one tittle shall in no wise pass from the law till all be fulfilled.*" Matt. v. 17, 18.

The names, *Scripture, the Law and the Prophets, the Law, the Prophets, and the Psalms,* employed by our Saviour, were familiar to Jewish ears, and covered the entire volume of Old Testament writings. The words of Jesus which we have just quoted put the stamp of infallibility upon the Hebrew Bible.

(4.) *Verbal references to the Old Testament.*

If the evidence which has been already advanced is not considered strong enough to shut out the possibility of any error in the Old Testament, let it be noticed that we have the most emphatic testimony to the infallibility of its very *words*. On a single word in the Old Testament our Saviour based his reply to those who denied the doctrine of the resurrection: " But as touching the resurrection of the dead, have ye not read that which was spoken unto you by God, saying, I AM the God of Abraham, and the God of Isaac, and the God of Jacob? God is not the God of the dead, but of the living." Matt. xxii. 31, 32.

In defending himself from the charge of blasphemy, he makes use of a single word in the eighty-second Psalm: "Jesus answered them, Is it not written in your law, I said ye are gods? If he called them gods to whom the word of God came, and the Scripture cannot be broken, say ye of him whom the Father hath sanctified and sent into the world, Thou blasphemest, because I said I am the Son of God?" John x. 34. Our Saviour justifies in parenthesis his appeal to this expression in the eighty-second Psalm, by reminding his hearers of the infallibility of the Scriptures. The passage is of great value in the discussion of the subject of inspiration, for it shows that our Saviour considered that not the thoughts merely, but the language also, of Holy Writ possessed divine authority, since he made the solemn utterance, *And the Scriptures cannot be broken*, in order to justify an argument based on a single word.

Notice the instances in which the correspondence between Old Testament prediction and New Testament fulfilment depends on *single words*. We may refer to the " thirty pieces of silver," the " potter's field," " the parting of the garments," as illustrations. If we are prepared to say that these allusions were regarded by the sacred writers as only remarkable coincidences, we should not allow them much weight in the argument. But inasmuch as the New Testament was written by men divinely commissioned, we must suppose that the writers were honest in what they say, and competent therefore to speak on the subject. Their mention of these incidents in our Lord's life as fulfilments of the Old Testament predictions must be regarded as proof that the divine agency employed in the composition of Scripture extended even to the choice of words.

Let us turn to the Epistles of Paul, and we shall find that verbal quotations from the Old Testament are extensively employed by that apostle for argumentative purposes. "St Paul rests his proof that the Jews as well as the Gentiles were concluded under sin on two little words occurring in the fourteenth Psalm — on the word 'none' in the first verse, and on the word 'all' in the third. Let these two little words be changed, and the apostle's argument falls at once. . . . . He teaches the equality of all men before God, and the freedom of this divine mode of saving, on the authority of a single emphatic word used by the prophet Joel — 'whosoever.' On this word he elaborately argues, Rom x. 12: 'There is no difference between the Jew and the Greek, for the same Lord over all is rich unto all that call upon him.' Then comes the authority for the assertion:

'For *whosoever* shall call upon the name of the Lord shall be saved.' .... In arguing in Gal. iii. 16, that the promise of eternal life is annexed to faith and not to human merit, he argues not alone from a single word, but from a single letter— from the fact that a word is used in the singular, not in the plural, ' He saith not, And to seeds, as of many, but as of one, and to thy *seed*, which is Christ.' "*

Some writers see in these citations only evidences of false reasoning on the part of the apostles. And we must confess that if the quotations from the Old Testament are the words of mere human authors, they have been adduced with unpardonable looseness. Unless the words of the Old Testament are invested with divine authority, it will be difficult to escape the conviction that the most weighty conclusions have been based on very frivolous premises. But we know too much of Paul's honesty and Paul's logic to charge him with such argumentative unfairness, and because we cannot take the position of the skeptic, we are obliged to conclude that these citations give the strongest testimony to the verbal infallibility of the whole Old Testament. I say, of *the whole Old Testament*, for there

* Garbett, p. 312.

is no reason for supposing that these passages which have been cited occupy a different rank from others which have received no special mention. Besides, we must remember that the apostle's reasoning proceeds on this assumption. A premise is suppressed in his argument, and that is the admitted infallibility of the Scriptures. Single words are available for purposes of argument, *because they are contained in the Scriptures.* Deny the verbal infallibility of the Old Testament as a whole, and it will be impossible for us to attach much importance to arguments based on particular passages.

(5.) *Direct assertions of divine authorship.*

The best—I may say, the only—way of accounting for the absolute authority which we find the words of Scripture to possess, is to suppose that the sacred writers were influenced in their choice of language by the divine mind. Having proved the verbal infallibility of the Old Testament, its divine authorship seems to follow as a necessary consequence. At all events, very little Scripture testimony will be sufficient to make the argument for plenary inspiration conclusive.

There are two passages which give testimony to the divine authorship of the Old Testament, from the singular use of the word Scripture. Thus we read, Rom. ix. 17: "For the Scripture saith unto Pharaoh, Even for this same purpose have I raised thee up, that I might show my power in thee, and that my name might be declared throughout the earth." Gal. iii. 8: "The Scripture, foreseeing that God would justify the heathen through faith, preached before the gospel unto Abraham, saying, In thee shall all nations be blessed." These passages are not parallel to those in which Scripture is personified and quotations are prefaced with the words, "Thus saith the Scripture." Here it is represented as saying what was said by God, of doing what was done by God, of wearing attributes which belong only to God. This can be explained only by the supposition that the apostle was so thoroughly convinced that the words of the Old Testament are the utterances of God that Scripture is identified with its author, and the acts of the latter are represented as being done by the former. There are passages, particularly in the Epistle to the Hebrews, in which the words of Scripture are quoted as those of God. Heb. i. 5: "For unto which of the angels said he at any time, Thou art my Son?" and verse 7: "And of the angels he saith." Verse 8: "But unto the Son he saith." viii. 8: 'For finding fault with them, he saith."

Verse 13: "In that he saith, A new covenant, he hath made the first old." This mode of citation, which is peculiar to the Epistle to the Hebrews, is a strong testimony to the divine authorship of the Old Testament. The Scriptures must have been regarded as equivalent to the utterances of God, or there would have been no propriety in making quotations from them with the preface, "*He saith,*" instead of, "*It is written.*"

Again, passages are cited from the Scriptures as the words of the Holy Ghost. Heb. iii. 7: "Wherefore, as the Holy Ghost saith, To-day, if ye will hear his voice, harden not your hearts," etc. Heb. x. 15: "Whereof the Holy Ghost also is a witness to us: for after that he had said before, This is the covenant that I will make with them after those days, saith the Lord; I will put my laws into their hearts, and in their minds will I write them," etc. The union of the divine and human agencies in the composition of Scripture is set forth in the following quotations: Acts iv. 24: "And when they heard that, they lifted up their voice to God with one accord and said, Lord, thou art God who hast made heaven and earth, and the sea and all that in them is, *who, by the mouth of thy servant David, hast said,* Why did the heathen rage and the people imagine a vain thing?" Acts i. 16: "And in those days Peter stood up in the midst of the disciples and said, ... Men and brethren, *this Scripture must needs have been fulfilled which the Holy Ghost, by the mouth of David, spake* before concerning Judas," etc.

There are two passages which directly assert the inspiration of the Old Testament. 2 Pet. i. 20: " Knowing this first, that no prophecy of the Scripture is of any private interpretation. For the prophecy came not in old time by the will of man, but holy men of old *spake as they were moved by the Holy Ghost.*" 2 Tim. iii. 15, 16: "And that from a child thou hast known *the holy Scriptures* (τὰ ἱερὰ γράμματα), which are able to make thee wise unto salvation through faith, which is in Christ Jesus. *All Scripture is given by inspiration of God,*" etc. (πᾶσα γραφὴ θεόπνευστος). This passage, viewed in the light of the foregoing evidence, must be regarded as conclusive testimony to the plenary inspiration of the Old Testament.

It will not affect the argument to translate this passage, All Scripture is given by inspiration, or every Scripture given by inspiration of God is profitable. The reference in either case is to the whole Old Testament, alluded to in the previous verse as the holy Scriptures—ἱερὰ γράμματα. If the first translation is a correct one, the passage is an assertion of inspiration on the part of the apostle. If the second be the true rendering, inspiration is alluded to as an admitted truth, and made the ground for the assertion that the Scriptures are able to make wise unto salvation. However translated, the passage must be regarded as testimony to the theopneustic character of the Hebrew Scriptures. Aside from the evidence which we have already considered, we could not rest a very positive argument on this single passage, for discussion might arise on the exact meaning of the word θεόπνευστος. This expression must be interpreted in the light of the foregoing evidence. The conclusions we have already reached may be fairly used to help us in our attempt to define its meaning; for this meaning, whatever it be, must be compatible with the facts already discovered. We find that the Scriptures give evidence of the presence of the divine mind in their composition; that the New Testament writers regarded the Old Testament as infallible, and rest elaborate arguments on single words taken from its pages; that passages are quoted as the utterances of God, and that others are ascribed to the Holy Ghost as the author of them. In asserting, therefore, that the Old Testament is *theopneustic*—God-breathed—the apostle must have meant that the sacred writers were influenced even in their choice of words by the Holy Ghost.

"The New Testament canonizes the Old; the INCARNATE WORD sets his seal on the WRITTEN WORD. The Incarnate Word is God—therefore, the inspiration of the Old Testament is authenticated by God himself."* The testimony to the inspiration of the New Testament is, we confess, less explicit and not so abundant. We might expect this to be the case, from the simple fact that God's message was *completed* in the writings of the New Testament. The apostles were the legitimate successors of the prophets, and, as such, gave ample testimony to their inspiration; but the apostles themselves had no successors. Besides, when the inspiration of the Old Testament is established, but little evidence is needed to warrant the inference that the New is likewise inspired. The Old and New Testaments are parts of the same divine message. They constitute a progressive unity; they exhibit the development of a single plan of salvation. Can we suppose that the Old Testament is

* Wordsworth on the Canon, p. 51, Am. ed.

God's word and the New Testament only man's word? Are the Gospels human productions, while the Pentateuch is an inspired writing? The presumption in favor of the inspiration of the New Testament is so strong that only very decided evidence to the contrary could make us doubt it. It must be borne in mind that the gift of inspiration was distinctly promised by our Saviour to his disciples: "When they bring you unto the synagogues and unto magistrates and powers, take ye no thought how or what thing ye shall answer or what ye shall say: for the Holy Ghost shall teach you in the same hour what ye ought to say." Luke xii. 11, 12. "When they shall lead you and deliver you up, take no thought beforehand what ye shall speak, neither do ye premeditate; but whatsoever shall be given you in that hour, that speak ye: for it is not ye that speak, but the Holy Ghost." Mark xiii. 11. "Settle it therefore in your heart not to meditate before what ye shall answer: for I will give you a mouth and wisdom which all your adversaries shall not be able to gainsay nor resist." Luke xxi. 14. The apostles, moreover, claimed to speak by divine guidance: "I say the truth in Christ; I lie not; my conscience also bearing me witness in the Holy Ghost." Romans ix. 1. "Which things also we speak, not in words which man's wisdom teacheth, but in words which the Holy Ghost teacheth, comparing spiritual things with spiritual" (1 Cor. ii. 13—πνευματικοῖς πνευματικὰ συγκρίνοντες) "joining spiritual things to spiritual words." See Hodge on 1 Cor. *in loc.* "I told you before, and foretell you, as if I were present, the second time; and being absent now I write to them who heretofore have sinned and to all other, that if I come again I will not spare, since ye seek a proof of *Christ speaking in me* which to youward is not weak, but is mighty in you." 2 Cor. xiii. 2, 3. It may be said, however, that these passages, after all, only prove that the apostles were inspired in their *oral* utterances. But would they be inspired *to speak* and not be inspired *to write?* Is it likely that if they were inspired when called before a human tribunal, they were left to the exercise of their fallible judgment in composing the books which should nourish the faith of God's people in every age? Certainly Paul did not suppose that so wide a difference existed between his oral and his written instructions when he said to the Thessalonians, "Stand fast and hold the traditions which ye have been taught, whether *by word or our epistle.*" 2 Thess. ii. 15.

With the quotation of a single passage from the

Second Epistle of Peter we shall close the evidence on the question of New Testament inspiration. It is one in which the Epistles of Paul are recognized as co-ordinate in point of authority with the Old Testament writings: "Even as our beloved brother Paul also, according to the wisdom given unto him, hath written unto you, as also in all his epistles, speaking in them of these things, in which are some things hard to be understood, which they that are unlearned and unstable wrest as they do also the *other* Scriptures unto their own destruction." 2 Pet. iii. 15-17.

We are led, as the result of our inquiries, to the irresistible conclusion that the books of the Bible —constituting, as they do, a unity; contributing severally to the development of a single scheme of divine grace; claiming to be a message to men from God; speaking in terms of authority concerning duty and destiny—were composed by men who acted under the influence of the Holy Ghost to such an extent that they were preserved from every error of fact, of doctrine, of judgment; and these so influenced in their choice of language that the words they used were the words of God. This is the doctrine which is known as that of PLENARY VERBAL INSPIRATION.

CHAPTER VI.

OBJECTIONS CONSIDERED.

ATHEISM or Christianity is the alternative which an infidel philosophy offers the world. The controversy between Christian and anti-Christian thought must therefore turn upon the question regarding the divine authority of the Bible. Hence it is not difficult to account for the growing skepticism throughout Christendom with regard to the plenary inspiration of the Scriptures.

There is, of course, a very wide difference between those who hold imperfect views of inspiration and those who deny it altogether. Some take the extreme pantheistic position that a revelation is impossible; some resolve inspiration into genius, and allow that Isaiah and Paul were inspired in the sense that Homer and Shakespeare were. Some are advocates of a partial inspiration, and are willing to concede that the doctrines of the Bible were infallibly recorded through divine agency, while they hold that the writers were left to the exercise of their ordinary faculties in selecting and recording the facts. Some have no difficulty in supposing that the *thoughts* were suggested to the sacred writers by the Holy Ghost, while they were left to the exercise of their unassisted powers in clothing them with words. However wide the differences which separate these classes of men, they agree in denying that *all* the parts of the Bible were written by men under the influence of the Holy Ghost in such a sense that the words of Scripture are the words of God. Even men who stand high in theological circles embrace a theory of inspiration which tolerates mistakes on the part of the sacred writers. Fairness, therefore, demands that we give due attention to the difficulties which are said to encumber this doctrine.

Before entering upon a consideration of the objections, I would remind the reader that the present attitude of thought is alarmingly Rationalistic. There is a growing disposition to make human reason the standard of truth. "The infallibility of private opinion is, with many, a far more palatable doctrine than the infallibility of the Bible." Hence, the readiness, and in many cases the delight, with which men find objections to the doctrine under discussion. It is a noticeable fact that in the doctrinal controversies of the day, the so-called *rational* argument is employed by those who reject the truth far more than the argument from Scripture. Men take the element of guilt out of sin, the element of satisfaction out of the atonement, the element of justice out of God's nature, on the ground of certain preconceived opinions with regard to the relations we sustain to God. The opponents of the doctrines of the Church do not rest their case on exegetical grounds, but the Scripture, when it is used at all, is employed mainly to lend the appearance of support to a foregone conclusion. The real argument, however disguised, is, "This is my opinion."

Let us now notice briefly the main objections which have been urged against the doctrine of inspiration.

(1.) *Revelation said to be impossible.*

The first class of objectors are those who forestall all inquiry by the assertions that a revelation is impossible. This objection has weight only on the supposition that there is no God. But if a man adopts a philosophy which leads to Atheism, the only way to answer his objection is to upset his philosophy. Suppose the question were asked, Given the universal belief of mankind in the existence of God, can we vindicate that belief? And this in my judgment is really the fair way of presenting the question concerning the being of God. How should we proceed? We could not take a single step in settling this question unless we had correct views on a fundamental question in psychology. To establish the doctrine of Theism it is necessary to vindicate the authority of primary beliefs. Now, consciousness is the common material out of which philosophy of every complexion is made. Men differ in their interpretations of consciousness, while they admit that her authority is unquestionable. All agree that consciousness testifies to the distinction answering to the words subject and object, *ego* and *non ego*. We cannot think, feel or will without realizing this distinction. The question arises, Is the distinction ultimate? Can we trust our intuitive conviction? The battle-ground of the rival philosophies is just here. It may be said that there is no real ground for the distinction between self and not self, but (1) what we call the "not self" is only the necessary modification of the mind; in which case our logical landing-place is a system of idealistic Pantheism. Or (2) that what we call "self" is only a modification of matter; in which case we fall into unqualified Materialism. I am stating a well-known fact in the history of opinion when I say that the pantheistic character of the post-Kantian philosophy of Germany is attributable to the denial of the fundamental distinction between subject and object to which consciousness testifies. The materialistic character of the Positive Philosophy, represented by such men as J. S. Mill, Bain, Herbert Spencer, has its root in the same psychological error. It is unnecessary for me to repeat the arguments by which Sir William Hamilton demonstrated the duality of consciousness as an ultimate fact in our constitution. What I have said will be sufficient to show how intimately the philosophical questions of the day are connected with fundamental doctrines of the Christian system. The objection that a revelation is impossible grows out of a false philosophy, which, by denying the validity of our primary beliefs, leads to Atheism. Granted that there is a God, it is absurd to say that he cannot reveal himself.

(2.) *The Bible said to contradict science.*

Truth cannot contradict truth. We cannot resist the conclusions which have been fairly arrived at by scientific men. We cannot resist the evidence that the Bible is the word of God. The discrepancies, therefore, between Scripture statements and the theories of science prove either that we have misinterpreted Scripture or that the scientific theories are untrue. Sometimes it may be necessary to modify our translation of the Bible in the light of scientific discovery. Science, therefore, ought to be, and has been, an exegetical help. Inspiration must not be held responsible for our erroneous interpretations. The discoveries of geology have thrown light upon the first chapter of Genesis, but whatever theory be adopted for the purpose of harmonizing the two accounts of the early history of our planet, the inspiration of Genesis is unaffected.

It is asking too much, however, when we are required to accommodate our interpretation of Scripture to a theory which is still a matter of debate among scientific men. We cannot give up the Scripture account of the creation on the ground that it does not agree with Darwin's theory of the origin of species, for the simple reason that on scientific ground Darwinianism has been proved to be untrue. The objection that the sacred writers are destitute of astronomical knowledge, and that their language is in accordance with an unscientific age, when men believed that the earth was a flat surface and that the heavenly bodies actually moved as they appeared to an observer on the earth, is too obviously foolish to need refutation. "The purpose of holy Scripture," says Baronius, " is to teach us how to go to heaven, and not how the heavens go."* The Bible was not intended as a text-book in science, and we have no right to expect that it should anticipate the discoveries of a thousand years. It was intended for the ignorant and the learned alike, and in order that it might be understood it was necessary that events should be described in the language of every-day life. No charge of scientific inaccuracy can damage the authority of the Scriptures, when it is remembered that the teaching of science forms no part of the object for which they were given. And the accuracy of Scripture is sufficiently vindicated when it is shown that in describing phenomena in the language of every-day life it teaches no error. This has been done again and again.

(3.) *The Bible said to contradict itself.*

As early as the time of Celsus, in the second century, the discrepancies which are found in the Bible, especially in the evangelists, were made use of as arguments against the divine authority of the Scriptures, and at the present day are sources of anxiety to many who cannot be accused of any desire to find objections to inspiration. The following are

* Quoted by Guizot, Meditations, 1st Ser., p. 187. Am. ed.

some of the alleged instances of contradiction: In the accounts of the cure of the centurion's servant, Matthew (viii. 5-13) states the centurion came to Jesus, while Luke (vii. 1-10) says that he sent first the elders of the Jews and then his friends. There are three accounts of the curing of blindness at Jericho. Matthew (xx. 30) mentions that there were two blind men, Mark (x. 46) and Luke (xviii. 35) mention only one. Matthew and Mark say the miracle was performed when Jesus was going out of Jericho—Luke, when he was coming in. Matthew (viii. 28), relating the incident of the demoniacs at Gadara, states that there were two men who met Jesus, while Mark (v. 2) mentions only one. Similar discrepancies are alleged to exist in the accounts which we have of our Lord's infancy and of his resurrection, as well as of the inscription on the cross. The same objection is also raised with reference to the twofold record of the sermon on the mount.

How are we to meet this objection? In the first place, we must remember that the inspiration of the Scriptures has already been established by the most abundant evidence. That being the case, we are safe in assuming that these apparent contradictions are only apparent. Any hypothesis which will harmonize the discrepancies must be considered a fair answer to the objection. This principle would be considered valid in any other department of inquiry, and its application here ought not to be objected to. If, for example, certain phenomena in nature were observed which apparently contradicted the law of gravitation, the scientific student would feel that any hypothesis should be accepted which would explain the contradiction, and if none could be suggested, rather than give up the established doctrine of gravitation, he would be willing to wait until further discovery should throw light upon the subject. With regard to most of the alleged discrepancies to be found in Scripture the method of harmonizing is very simple.

One hundred and forty-four passages are reconciled by the application of this simple rule given by Mr. Garbett :* "*Variations of statements are not contradictions when they arise either from recording different parts of some common event, or from assigning a different emphasis and importance to the same parts.*" Take the case of the centurion, above quoted. Luke's statement does not contradict Matthew's, unless we suppose that each intended to tell the whole story. There is nothing unnatural in the supposition that he sent first the elders, and

* Go l's Word Written, p. 267.

then his friends, and that finally, through anxiety for his servant, he came himself. Take the case of the angels at the sepulchre; Matthew and Mark mention one, Luke says there were two. The accounts are not irreconcilable. Matthew related the appearance of the angel in connection with the rolling away of the stone. It was enough for his purpose to mention one. Mark mentions the angel who addressed the women. His silence with regard to the presence of another does not contradict Luke's account. We cannot bring the charge of contradiction against the evangelists in these and similar instances, unless we adopt the rule that truthfulness in the report of the same occurrence by different persons is inconsistent with circumstantial variations.

Mr. Garbett gives another very important rule: "*Separate transactions are not to be identified with each other because of a parallelism between some circumstances of an event or some portions of a discourse.*"

When Mark states that Jesus cured a blind man when he went out of Jericho, he clearly contradicts Luke, who relates that the cure was performed when he was going into Jericho--*provided the two accounts refer to the same event.* But the discrepancy is easily removed by the supposition that the evangelists relate two distinct miracles. If there remain passages which we cannot reconcile, we must conclude that the discrepancies arise out of the absence of the historical links which would show their connections. It would be unfair, after all the evidence we have for the inspiration of the Scriptures, to charge the same writers with glaring contradictions, because from our defective information we are unable to harmonize their statements. Says Dr. Lee: "It has been reserved for modern times to suggest a solution which has been almost universally accepted, and which removes every shade of difficulty from the case. Mark asserts that our Lord was crucified 'at the third hour,' or at nine o'clock in the forenoon; while according to John, Pilate about the sixth hour was still sitting in judgment. The explanation of this apparent discordance in time—an explanation which even Strauss, while exaggerating 'the difficulty' to the utmost, allows to be 'possible'—is, that John has given the hour according to the Roman calculation of time, which counted as we do from midnight; while Mark adheres to the Jewish custom of counting from sunrise." Closer study of the Scriptures, and increased knowledge of subjects cognate to these inquiries, we may well hope, will clear up many difficulties which now serve to try our faith.

(4.) *Unimportant passages.*

Some men shrink from the doctrine of plenary inspiration lest they should be compelled to believe that Paul sent his salutations to Tryphena and Tryphosa, and gave special instructions concerning the cloak which he left at Troas, while writing under the influence of the Spirit. I have not space to dwell upon the importance of these so-called insignificant details. If I could show, as Gaussen has beautifully shown,* how vividly in these passages the apostle is presented to us in the circumstances of his daily life; if I could show that these passages complained of are the modest witnesses to the self-sacrifice of Paul; if I could show that they are expressions of the tenderness of his nature, of his affectionate regard for those who have ministered to him; if I could show that these passages contain vivid pictures of the relations sustained by the members of the primitive Church to each other; if I could show that these salutations, said to be unworthy of inspiration, are suggestive of the lesson that Christianity ought to

* Gaussen on Inspiration, p. 186, American edition.

manifest itself in Christian courtesy and a delicate consideration of the wants of others,—then I think the objection that these so-called insignificant passages are unworthy of a place in a volume of inspired writings would fall to the ground.

(5.) *Objections based on* 1 Cor. chapter vii.

In the sixth verse of this chapter Paul says, "I speak this by permission, not of commandment." It is argued that the apostle here clearly distinguishes the words which he spoke by divine authority from those which he uttered in the exercise of his own judgment. The difficulty is entirely removed by a more correct translation. He is teaching not that there are some things which he is permitted to say, and some which he speaks by commandment, but that his recommendation was not given in the way of positive *command*, but of *allowance:* "I say this by way of allowance for you, not by way of command."

Again, in verse 10, he says, "Unto the married I command, yet not I, but the Lord;" verse 12: "But to the rest speak I, not the Lord;" verse 25: "Now, concerning virgins, I have no commandment of the Lord, yet I give my judgment."

"By which language," says Lee,* "he is supposed

* Inspiration, p. 272.

to intimate that this certain point of Scripture the author may write according to his own uninspired human judgment, although guided in other portions of his work by the Holy Ghost. Such an inference, however, is altogether at variance with Paul's design, whose words in this case can only be distorted into an argument against inspiration by utterly overlooking his object and meaning. The first of the three expressions which have been quoted, 'I command, yet not I, but the Lord,' obviously refers to the institution by Christ (as Mark has recorded the circumstances) of the original law of marriage, and relates to an ordinance revealed from the very first and obligatory on every occasion and in every age; while, by the two latter passages—on which the argument against inspiration rests—Paul, as the context clearly proves, merely intends to convey that Christ had directly provided for those particular cases in which his apostle now pronounces his inspired and authoritative opinion."

I have noticed the main objections to the doctrine of plenary inspiration. There are others which arise out of a misunderstanding of the doctrine, and some of these will be considered in the next chapter.

OBJECTIONS CONSIDERED.

It is but fair that we should now ask those who maintain a theory of partial inspiration what proof they have to offer in support of it? Our conclusions, if they have been fairly reached, throw upon those who differ with us the burden of proving their position. We find nothing in the Bible to favour a theory which labels one part of it as God's work and another as man's. We have a right, therefore, to say to him who holds such an opinion, " Your theory presupposes that you are able to put your finger on certain passages of Scripture and say, These are divine, and on certain other passages and say, These are human. Only by your ability to discriminate between what is man's and what is God's in the Bible can you save your theory from the charge of *begging the question*. And if you profess to be able to make this discrimination, then we ask you to tell us the standard by which you are governed." In reply to this challenge we should doubtless be referred to a so-called "*verifying faculty*." Says the author of "Liber Librorum," "We now approach that portion of our task which demands of us '*a principle*,' by the help of which we may, without weakening our faith in Scripture as a whole, separate its parts and distinguish between that which is divine and that which is human.

We call this the 'verifying faculty,' and regard it as being neither more nor less than '*reason enlightened and sanctified by the Holy Ghost.*'"* "Reason," as Bishop Butler says, who is quoted by this author in the sentence following the above, "is the only faculty we have wherewith to judge concerning anything, even revelation itself." But there is a proper and an improper use of reason in matters of religion. When reason is exercised within her proper sphere, she has not a syllable to say against plenary inspiration. It is only when she has given her judgment in questions over which she has no jurisdiction, that objections have been raised against the doctrine.

Contradictions cannot be true, and inspiration could not make them credible. If the Bible is a bundle of contradictions, we may safely say that it did not come from a God of truth. But reason is going outside of her province when she brings the charge of contradiction against discrepant statements, simply because the means of reconciling them are not at hand. Again, the distinction between right and wrong is a moral intuition. God cannot do wrong. But it is clear that many things are right for God to do which would be wrong for

* Page 77.

men to do. It is wrong for a man to slay his neighbour, but who will dispute God's right to dispose of his creatures as he pleases? I do not affirm that justice means anything different with God from what it is with man. Whatever philosophy may say on the analogy between the human and the divine attributes, the believer in Scripture must consider the question settled, for "God made man in his own image." But the rights and obligations recognized among men grow out of the relations which men sustain to one another. To affirm that right and wrong between man and God are in all cases the same as right and wrong between man and man, is to affirm that the relations which subsist between man and his Maker are in all cases similar to those which subsist between man and his neighbour. The objections which are made to the doctrine of inspiration, on the score that certain passages in the Old Testament and certain doctrines in the New are incompatible with the character of God, are based on an attempt to narrow God to the limits of human relationship and bind him by the laws which govern human society.

There are certain intuitive truths which underlie every process of reasoning and are the basis of all religious faith. Let us take the two which we have already mentioned as illustrations—the law of contradiction in logic and the distinction between right and wrong in ethics. If we cannot rely upon the validity of these primary beliefs, we cannot pursue any argument or receive any revelation. Clearly, then, it is the province of reason to decide whether the Bible as a whole, or in any of its parts, contradicts any of our primary beliefs; and if it does, it is safe to say that the Bible, or a part of it, does not come from God. But we are not aware of any intuitive belief by which we can determine what is proper and what is not proper for God to do on every occasion; what passages in the Bible have sufficient dignity to be assigned to divine authorship and what have not; what occasions are important enough for the manifestation of God's miraculous power and what are not. And men have pushed the exercise of their blind, erring intellect to an unwarranted extent when they have undertaken to say what God ought or ought not to do, and what his word ought or ought not to contain.

When it is said that certain passages are too unimportant to be considered as inspired, it is fair to ask the objector if he can tell us what is the *minimum* of importance an inspired passage should possess. We confess to a lack in our mental constitution which incapacitates us from drawing a nice boundary line between the human and the divine, and prevents us from setting limits to the divine propriety. So with objections drawn from the style in which the books are written. The book of Job and the prophecies of Isaiah differ in style from the Acts of the Apostles and the Epistle to the Romans, but have we a right to say that one style is God's and the other man's? What do we know of God's *style?* This is not the place for me to speak of the individuality of the writers. I shall do so in the next chapter. In the mean time, it is sufficient to protest against the criticism which resolves inspiration into a question of æsthetics.

CHAPTER VII.

EXPLICATION OF THE DOCTRINE OF INSPIRATION.

IN recent discussions on the subject of inspiration, prominence has been given to some questions which as yet have not been alluded to in these pages. A consideration of them will be necessary for the purpose of defining with greater strictness the doctrine of inspiration, and of answering objections which arise out of a misapprehension of it.

(1.) *When it is claimed that the Scriptures are inspired, it must be understood that we refer to the original manuscripts.*

This remark is necessary in view of the objections which are based on the various readings of MSS. and on differences in translations. The books of the Bible as they came from the hands of their writers were infallible. The autographs were penned under divine guidance. It is not claimed that a perpetual miracle has preserved the sacred text from the errors of copyists. The inspired character of our Bible depends, of course, upon its correspondence with the original inspired manuscripts. These autographs are not in existence, and we must determine the correct text of Scripture in the same way that we determine the text of any of the ancient classics.

We are not in possession of an autograph copy of the "Æneid" or the "Ars Poetica," yet no one refuses to receive our editions of these poems as the genuine productions of Virgil and Horace. There is therefore no force in the objection against inspiration we are now considering, for just so far as our present Scripture text corresponds with the original documents is it inspired; and so far as any translation is a faithful rendering of the original does it possess the authority of an inspired document. Have we a correct text? If we have not, then just in proportion to its incorrectness are we without the word of God. Are the various readings of sufficient importance to shake our faith in the genuineness of our Scripture text? Let us take the testimony of those who have investigated the subject. Says Professor Moses Stuart: "Out of some eight hundred thousand various readings of the Bible that have been collected, about seven hundred and ninety-five thousand are of about as much importance to the sense of the Greek and

Hebrew Scriptures as the question in English orthography is, whether the word *honour* shall be spelled with a *u* or without it. Of the remainder, some change the sense of particular passages or expressions, or omit particular words or phrases; but no one doctrine of religion is changed, not one precept is taken away, not one important fact is altered, by the whole of the various readings collectively taken." Says Garbett: "Let every word affected by these variations be put on one side, not as certainly uninspired, but as not being certainly inspired, because it is not certainly identical with the original autographs. It will be quite enough if the verbal inspiration of all the rest be admitted. For this inspired portion, on which variation of reading has not thrown the shadow of a question, contains so entirely every expressive and emphatic word that the denial of inspiration to the remainder becomes simply nugatory, if it be not ridiculous."*

It may be said, "This admission materially weakens the argument. If you do not claim that the MSS. have been miraculously preserved from error in the transmission of them, why are you so strenuous in favour of a verbal inspiration?

* God's Word Written, p. 342.

What do you gain?" We gain all the difference there is between an inspired and an uninspired original. This difference is apparent. According to our view, an infallible autograph has been perpetuated by the industry of transcribers, and has been changed only in some unimportant details through the mistakes of copyists. According to the other view, similar changes have been incorporated in a document *faulty at the outset.* On the one supposition, Paul wrote his Epistle to the Romans under divine guidance, so that the doctrine of justification by faith is God's own commentary on the sacrifice of Christ; on the other, the epistle contains only the expression of Paul's individual opinion, or is at best a human version of a divine revelation, and came from Paul's hands with the defects of a purely human authorship.

(2.) *Inspiration is not claimed for the writers of Scripture in a sphere outside of their official work.*

The infallible communication of God's message, whether oral or written, was the design of inspiration. In the discharge of their official duties the apostles and prophets acted under the unerring guidance of the Holy Ghost. No objection against inspiration can be drawn from the fallibility which the writers of Scripture exhibit in private life.

Because God made the writers of Scripture infallible as the official communicators of his will, it does not follow that he made them perfect as men. We have reason to suppose that the Christian experience of the apostles was analogous to that of Christians in our day. Paul spoke with confidence concerning his preaching, but with great humility concerning his personal attainments in holiness. The Psalms of David are the inspired liturgy of the Church, but David had no inspiration to keep him from sin. Paul was inspired to write his epistles, but the gift of infallibility did not extend to a knowledge of what should befall him at Jerusalem. So we read that Peter "dissembled" at Antioch, and that there was a "sharp contention" between Paul and Barnabas. But these sins and failings with which the apostles were chargeable as private Christians should not be brought up as objections to their inspiration when they were acting in their official capacity. It is urged that this view of the inspiration under which the sacred writers acted breaks up the unity of their lives by dividing them into inspired and uninspired portions. There is no force, however, in the objection if there is evidence for the fact. There is conclusive evidence that inspiration does not extend to *all* the actions

EXPLICATION OF THE DOCTRINE. 117

of those who are the subjects of it, in that God has on more than one occasion made bad men the infallible communicators of his will. Balaam had no inspiration to keep him from sin, and yet, wicked as he was, God made him infallible in the utterance of his prophecy. The fair inference from the teaching of Scripture is, that in their private life the sacred writers were under the ordinary influence of the Spirit of grace, and that they became the subjects of a specific influence the moment they opened their mouths to preach or took up their pens to write. So that their words, while in one sense their own, were also unequivocally God's.

(3.) *The specific agency of the Holy Ghost in rendering the sacred writers infallible in the communication of truth must not be confounded with his sanctifying influence on the hearts of all Christians.*

This mistake is commonly though inexcusably made, and arises from the fact that two specifically different operations of the Spirit are often called by the same name. Thus, in the communion service of the Church of England the prayer occurs, "that the thoughts of our hearts may be cleansed by the inspiration of the Holy Spirit, so that we may perfectly love God and worthily magnify his name." Mr. Maurice, after quoting this, adds: "Here are petitions which concern not a few specially religious men or some illuminated teachers, but all the miscellaneous people who are gathered together in a particular congregation. Are we paltering with words in a double sense? When we speak of inspiration, do we mean inspiration? When we refer to the inspiration of the Scriptures in our sermons, ought we to say, '.Brethren, we beseech you not to suppose that this inspiration at all resembles that for which you have been praying. They are generically, essentially unlike?'"

Mr. Maurice has written a very able history of philosophy, and is one of the leading thinkers in England to-day. He must have known that it is no uncommon thing for the same name to be used in a different sense. He must be familiar with what logicians call the *fallacia equivocationis*. Dr. Arnold fell into the same mistake. He says: "It is no less an unwarrantable interpretation of the word inspiration to suppose that it is equivalent to a communication of the divine perfections. Surely, many of our words and many of our actions are spoken and done by the inspiration of God's Spirit, without whom we can do nothing acceptable to God. Yet does the Holy Ghost so inspire us as to communicate to us his own perfections? Are our best words or works free from sin? All inspiration does not then destroy the human and fallible part in the nature which it inspires. It does not change men into God." *

Mr. Maurice says, in his Essay on Inspiration, " I shall fix my thoughts on the word *inspiration;* our disputes are emphatically about the word." The fallacy which underlies the writer's discussion of this subject is wrapped up in the sentence we have quoted. The controversy does not turn on the meaning of a word. The question is, whether the Bible is God's book or man's; whether the sacred writers were infallibly secured against error, or whether their writings are chargeable with the defects of merely human authorship. If the doctrine of an infallible rule of faith is proved, it makes little difference whether we call it inspiration or not. It is clear that the etymology of the word cannot settle the doctrine, but that the word must be defined by the doctrine which it is used to indicate. To illustrate: Human experience and the Bible teach that the sanctifying agency of the Spirit does not make man morally perfect. If, as in the Church of England Prayer-book, inspiration is the word used to express the sanctifying influ-

* Quoted by Lee, p. 217.

ence of the Spirit, then inspiration *in this sense* must be compatible with moral imperfections. Again, there is abundant evidence that the sacred writers, in the composition of Scripture, were made infallible by the special influence of the Holy Ghost. To express this agency we use the word inspiration, and used *in this sense* inspiration is certainly incompatible with error. It is just as idle to argue that the inspiration of the sacred writers did not render them infallible in the discharge of their official duties because the inspiration of private Christians does not make them perfect, as it would be to argue on the other side that every Christian under the inspiration of the Holy Ghost is morally perfect because infallibility is claimed on behalf of the writers of Scripture. How men of learning can be deceived by the ambiguous use of a word it is hard to imagine.

(4.) *Inspiration, though verbal, is not mechanical.*

It has been already shown that inspiration extends to the words of Scripture. When we say that the Scriptures are verbally inspired, we mean nothing more than that the writers were influenced in their choice of words by the Holy Ghost. We do not pretend to say *how* this influence was exerted. We certainly do not mean to say that the

EXPLICATION OF THE DOCTRINE. 121

words were *dictated,* or that the writers consciously acted as amanuenses. And yet there are those who seem to identify verbal inspiration with what is known as the mechanical theory. Thus Dr. Bannerman, in his very able work, says, "The theory of verbal inspiration, or the theory that human language was the medium through which the Holy Ghost both revealed truth to the prophet and empowered him to record it with infallible accuracy, is one that probably is not open to the objection of being inconsistent with the exercise of the faculties of the writers according to their ordinary laws. .... Still, it is a theory. ..... The connection between human thought and human language is not of that invariable kind to justify us in saying that there can be no access to the mind except through words, and no channel by which it can be guided to an infallible expression of them except a verbal inspiration." Using the expression, verbal inspiration, as Dr. Bannerman does, I fully concur with what he says. We certainly have no evidence that words are the only channel of communication between the Infinite and the finite mind. This is another instance in which the meaning of the word must be defined by the doctrine which it is employed to indicate. The writers of Scripture communicated God's message infallibly in words. The expression verbal inspiration implies that the inspiration of the sacred Scriptures extended to the words of Scripture. It does not mean that words were the channel through which the Spirit gained access to the minds of the sacred writers. It does not imply that the sacred writers were machines, or that they were the mere transcribers of words, which were successively whispered in their ears. The theory of verbal inspiration does not refer to the *process* by which the matter of Scripture was communicated to the writers, but to the *result* of the Spirit's influence as seen in an infallible writing. *How* the words of Scripture originated in the minds of the writers we do not know, but that they are God's words we do know, and therefore we say that the Bible is verbally inspired.

(5.) *There is a difference between revelation and inspiration.*

The reality of this distinction is not questioned, but the difficulty in fixing a boundary line between revelation and inspiration has given rise to a controversy between the ablest defenders of the infallibility of the Scriptures. A revelation is a supernatural communication of truth on the part of

God. This definition is accurate enough for our present purpose: we shall have occasion after a little to employ one that is more discriminating.

Now, the Bible, particularly the Old Testament, is full of recorded revelations which God from time to time made to his servants. The possession of a revelation, however, did not qualify a man for being the infallible instructor of others. He was liable to make mistakes and incorporate human errors in God's message. Hence, when God designed his communications to serve a public purpose, he not only gave revelations to his servants, but he rendered them infallible in communicating them through the influence of the Holy Spirit. Inspiration was the influence under which the sacred writers became infallible in the communication of truth to their fellow-men. This definition, however, though true, is not complete, and is liable to the objection that it only provides against the possibility of error on the part of the sacred writers, but does not give the character of divine authorship to their writings. It would be better to say that we understand the inspiration under which the Scriptures were written to mean that intimate relation between the Holy Spirit and the minds of the sacred writers in virtue of which we are justified in saying that the words of Scripture are the words of God. It is clear, then, that revelation does not imply inspiration. Joseph was warned of God in a dream. He received a revelation, but was not inspired. But does inspiration imply revelation? This has been a subject of discussion of late, particularly between Dr. Lee and Dr. Bannerman.

It is evident that in this controversy two very different questions have been confounded, to wit: (1.) The character in which the Bible *addresses us*, as the result of the labours of the sacred writers; and (2.) the manner in which the writers themselves derived the information which is recorded in the pages of Scripture. The first is evidently in Dr. Bannerman's mind when he says:

"It is somewhat startling to be told, not by the opponents, but by the friends of inspiration, that the Acts of the Apostles, and other such historical portions of the Bible, are no part of the revelation of God."

Again: "Had the prophets, or the evangelists, or the apostles the supernatural commission and gift of God to write in his name? This is the question which, if answered in the affirmative, gives to all they wrote the character of revelation."

Again: "If all the books, and all the parts of each book, uncorrupted and unmutilated, which are usually accounted to belong to the canon, have a right to their place there, it is impossible, without playing fast and loose with the evidence that accredits all alike, to deny to one portion the character of revelation while assigning it to the remainder." These remarks would have been just if, as Dr. Bannerman seems to have supposed, Dr. Lee had cast discredit upon the historical portions of the Scripture by denying their divine authorship. He has been led into this line of reasoning by a misapprehension of the real question at issue. If the question be put, Is the Bible a revelation to us from God? we answer, "*Yes—in all its parts*," since the words of Scripture are the words of God. But if we are asked whether all the contents of the Bible are the records of supernatural communications objectively presented to the minds of the writers, it will not be so easy to give an affirmative answer.

Let it be understood, then, that we are not now discussing the question whether the Bible comes to us in the character of a revelation from God. That is settled. The question is, whether there is such a difference in the way the sacred writers came into possession of the knowledge which they have embodied in the Scripture that we are justified in saying that in some cases they received their information by direct revelation from God, while in other cases they derived it from ordinary sources. In reply to this question, Dr. Lee answers yes; Dr. Bannerman, no.

It is of the first importance to determine, if possible, the exact meaning of a revelation. In all the revelations recorded in Scripture their objective character is unmistakable. A palpable distinction is preserved between the revealer, the thing revealed and the person receiving the revelation. Noah was warned of the deluge. The revelation took the most definite shape: "God said unto Noah, The end of all flesh is come before me; for the earth is filled with violence through them: and behold, I will destroy them with the earth. Make thee an ark of gopher wood: rooms shalt thou make in the ark," etc. Gen. vi. 13. God talked with Abram when he gave him the covenant of promise: "After these things the word of the Lord came unto Abram in a vision, saying, Fear not, Abram, I am thy shield and thy exceeding great reward. And he brought him forth abroad and said, Look now toward heaven and tell the stars, if thou be able to number them; and he said unto him, So shall thy seed be." The same distinctness characterizes the revelation which Daniel records in the ninth chapter of his prophecy: "Yea, while I was speaking in prayer, even the man Gabriel, whom I had seen in the vision at the beginning, being caused to fly swiftly, touched me about the time of the evening oblation. And he informed me and talked with me, and said, O Daniel, I am now come forth to give thee skill and understanding. .... Know, therefore, that from the going forth of the commandment to restore and build Jerusalem unto the Messiah the Prince shall be seven weeks and threescore and two weeks; the street shall be built again and the wall, even in troublous times." In the accounts which we have of the revelations given to Paul on his way to Damascus, and to Peter on the housetop at Joppa, the same sharp discrimination between the giver and the receiver of the communication is preserved. See Acts ix.; x. Turn finally to the account of the revelation given to John: "The revelation of Jesus Christ, which God gave unto him to show to his servants things that must shortly come to pass, and he sent and signified by his angel unto his servant John. .... I was in the spirit on the Lord's day, and heard behind me a great voice as a trumpet. .... And when I saw him I fell at his feet as dead, and he laid his right hand upon me, saying, Fear not," e c. Rev. i. etc.

The accounts we have cited are sufficient to afford material for an accurate definition of a revelation. In the Scripture sense of the term, a revelation means something more than that a conception has originated in the mind through divine agency; for not only in the cases cited was the matter of revelation a communication from God, but it was *known* to be so. The distinction between God communicating and the person receiving was as much a matter of consciousness as is the distinction between the object seen and the person seeing in an act of vision. If every thought which entered the mind of the sacred writers through divine influence is a revelation in the strict and proper sense of the word, there need be no hesitation in saying that everything in the Bible was communicated to the writers by special revelation. For whether they wrote history or doctrine—whether they searched records or made drafts on memory; whether they made statements with the preface, "Thus saith the Lord," or wrote what was a matter of general knowledge—in every case their conceptions were shaped, their words chosen, their selections made under the infallible guidance of the Holy Ghost.

But a revelation, as I have already said, means more than that a conception has originated in the mind through divine agency. It implies that truth has been *objectively* presented to the mind by dream, vision or audible voice, and *that its reception has been attended with the consciousness that it came from God.* Take, for example, the vision of Paul (Acts xvi. 9) which influenced him to go to Macedonia. How did he know that it was not a mere subjective state? And why did he feel bound to obey it? Simply because consciousness testified as clearly as to his own identity that he had been in direct communication with God.

Now the question is, Have we evidence that everything whatever the sacred writers penned was a revelation *in the sense defined?* Do we know, for example, that Paul could say, "These facts, these doctrines, this line of argument, this metaphor, these words which I have embodied in my epistle, were presented to my mind by direct communication from God, so that, in recording them, I am acting as his amanuensis, am reporting what God has said to me, am fixing on paper what God has made to pass before my mind"? I do not ask whether the apostles wrote under divine influence—this question has been already answered—or whether they knew that they were inspired; but have we evidence that they could always discriminate between the Holy Ghost as the communicator of truth and themselves as the recipients of it? Could they so objectify their conceptions as to be able to say, "These are revelations made to us by God"? If any such evidence exist, I am ignorant of it, and therefore, using the word revelation in this restricted sense, I cannot take the position with Dr. Bannerman, that revelation is co-extensive with inspiration. That this statement may not be understood as casting the slightest discredit upon the divine authorship and infallibility of the smallest portion of the Scriptures, let me ask the reader to remember the two senses in which the word revelation is used. Taking it in its wider sense, to express the idea that the Bible is a message to man from God for the guidance of life, we may say, with confidence every part of it is a revelation. Taking it in its narrower sense, to express the objective communication of truth by God to the sacred writers, we can only say that there is no evidence to warrant the assertion that everything incorporated in the Bible was first presented to the minds of the writers by means of revelations. Still, it is true that God may have presented the most familiar facts to the minds of the Scripture writers in a series of distinct revelations. We may think it unlikely that he would do so, but, for aught we know, he may have done so. Everything recorded in the Acts may have been revealed to Luke as distinctly, as objectively, as the vision which Peter saw when on the house-top in Joppa. Scripture furnishes no material for a positive answer to the question under discussion. We cannot affirm with Dr. Bannerman that revelation is co-extensive with inspiration. And on the other hand, we cannot, with Dr. Lee, be confident that it is not.

"But," says Dr. Bannerman, "without revelation in addition to inspiration, the utmost that can be said is, that the narrative is an infallible transcript or copy of the beliefs and knowledge of the writers, leaving it still an open question as to whether their beliefs and knowledge were true." Again: "The conception in the mind of the sacred penman, both of facts and truths, although recorded with infallible accuracy *as conceived*, may yet not answer to the reality."

If the office of inspiration is simply to enable the subjects of it to fix on paper their own conceptions with infallible accuracy, these remarks are just. It would be rather a useless inspiration, and one not worthy, we may say with reverence, of the Holy Spirit, which consisted only in stereotyping human errors and imperfections.

These remarks, however, are enough to show us at once the real point of difference between the two writers whose names have been so frequently mentioned. Dr. Bannerman limits inspiration to the infallible *expression* of thoughts, either orally or on paper. The *originating* of them in the minds of men is, in his view, the office of revelation. He narrows the sphere of inspiration, and is therefore led to widen the scope of revelation. According to the view which I have taken in these pages, the shaping of the conception in the mind of the sacred writer and its infallible communication in words are included under the idea of inspiration. According to Dr. Bannerman, the latter is the exclusive function of inspiration.

(6.) *There is a human and a divine element in the Scriptures.*

These adjectives are not used to distinguish different parts of the Bible. Nothing is implied in them disparaging to its plenary inspiration It is throughout a divine and a human book. In the strictest sense of the term, God is its author. And yet this is not equivalent to saying that God adopts every sentiment found in its pages. The Bible is not written throughout in the form of a direct address from God to men. Portions are so written, and portions embody the sentiments of men, and sometimes of very wicked men. Plenary inspiration does not involve the idea that God is responsible for these sentiments. It is a guarantee that they have been correctly rendered, but not that they have the divine sanction. Historians are not supposed to be in sympathy with all the wickedness they chronicle; and because God enabled his servants to transcribe with infallible accuracy the wicked and even blasphemous speeches of men, it does not follow that he endorses sin. Notice, too, the difference between the sentiments of inspired men, and an inspired account of the sentiments of men uninspired. Paul's judgment in reference to the question addressed to him by the Corinthians was infallible, because it was an inspired judgment. Job's friends, on the contrary, were not inspired, and though the writer of the book has given us an inspired account of what they said, their speeches do not on that account carry with them the divine approval. Coleridge therefore clearly misapprehended the nature of inspiration when he objected to the inspired character of the book of Job, because sentiments are therein expressed which are incompatible with the moral nature of God.

Again: the Bible is a human book. That is to say, it was written by men in human language. The sacred writers were not machines—were not mere amanuenses. Inspiration did not abridge their freedom or destroy their individuality. They were, in every sense of the word, authors. Differences of education, of character, of surrounding circumstances on the part of the several writers, give colouring to their books. "Where the prophet has been of the sacerdotal race, the various features of the theocracy—the temple and the altar, the ark and the cherubim—float before his view, as in the writings of Jeremiah and Ezekiel. The shepherd Amos still wanders in the pastures —his imagination still lingers with the flocks, and dwells on the culture of his fields—his similitudes are taken from the mildew which blights the vineyard or the lion which invades the fold." *

There is no difficulty in conceiving that the

* Lee on Inspiration, p. 173.

writers of Scripture reasoned, exercised memory, availed themselves even of existing documents, were free in the use of their faculties, while at the same time they were infallibly guided in the words they used by the Holy Ghost.

Let it be granted that inspiration did not destroy individuality, let it be admitted the sacred writers were truly the authors of the books they wrote, and we shall have no difficulty in accounting for variations in the accounts of the same event. Dean Alford finds an objection to the plenary inspiration of the Gospels in the different accounts of the inscription on the cross. Is it likely that four men relating the same event would use precisely the same language, or, reporting what had been said in their hearing, would do so without the omission, addition or change of a word? If in a court of justice four witnesses should give their testimony in precisely the same language, would the fact not afford a strong evidence of collusion. And is not diversity of statement within certain limits rather corroborative of truth than otherwise?

By placing the several statements of the evangelists side by side, we shall find that they are not contradictory, but that they differ only as they omit one or more of the words constituting the inscription. Thus:

The King of the Jews.—Mark.
This is the King of the Jews.—Luke.
This is Jesus, the King of the Jews.—Matthew.
Jesus of Nazareth, the King of the Jews.—John.

It was possible for the Spirit so to have influenced the evangelists that they should have reported this inscription *verbatim*. It was possible for the biographers of Christ, guided by inspiration, not to have varied a hair's breadth in their statements. But there are reasons which make it important that the individuality of the sacred writers should be preserved.

Suppose the whole Bible were in the form of a communication made by God to one man, and written by him with the preface, "Thus saith the Lord," how could we prove that its claims were valid? We should want the evidence of prophecy and its recorded fulfilment; we should miss the argument from the unity of design which we now have in a series of documents written by men who lived ages apart; we should be without the confirmatory testimony of One who wrought miracles in attestation of his divine commission. In short, we should be without the evidences which go to prove the divine authority of the Scriptures. The form which the Bible now possesses, it will not be rash to say, is essential. It is, among other reasons, because it comes to us as a series of *tracts* written by different men, yet pervaded by an unmistakable unity; it is because these tracts are so corroborative of each other that we are irresistibly led to a recognition of their historical value and divine authority. As has already been remarked, the Bible comes into the hands of the student as a series of literary documents. It must be judged as a human book. It cannot escape critical handling. It must be able to stand the ordeal of historical criticism before it can receive the homage of men as a divine revelation. Did Christ rise from the dead? We wish testimony to that effect—the independent testimony of those who saw him after his triumph over the grave—of Matthew, Mark, Luke and John.

Now it undoubtedly strengthens our faith in the evangelists—judging them as ordinary historians—to find in their pages essential agreement with circumstantial variety. In an *evidential* point of view it was a matter of great importance that the individuality of the writers of Scripture should be preserved, in order that the Bible might carry with it the unvarnished testimony of independent witnesses to the cardinal facts of the gospel. How much corroborative evidence concerning the life of Christ would be wanting if the four Gospels had been cast in one mould?

The Bible was written by men, and all that is ordinarily implied in human authorship (save fallibility) may be fairly ascribed to the sacred writers. The Bible was penned under the direct influence of the Holy Spirit, so that infallibility attaches to every word.

These two statements, placed side by side, constitute the sum of our knowledge concerning the composition of the Scriptures. We need not attempt to make a theory to explain how the human and the divine unite in the composition of the Scriptures. We do not know how the human and the divine unite in the person of Christ; we can only state the fact that Christ is "God and man in two distinct natures, and one person for ever." We do not know how the human and the divine unite in the process of sanctification. We know that a union of some kind is implied in Paul's address to the Philippians, "Work out your own salvation with fear and trembling: for it is God which worketh in you both to will and to do of his good pleasure."

The conclusion we reach on the subject which has been discussed in these pages is admirably expressed in the words of two recent writers. Says Westcott:* "We have a Bible competent to calm our doubts and speak to our weakness. It is authoritative, for it is the voice of God; it is intelligible, for it is in the language of men." Says Garbett:† "While the words of Scripture are truly and characteristically the words of men, they are at the same time fully and concurrently the words of God."

* Introduction to the Study of the Gospels, p. 33.
† God's Word Written, p. 293.

THE END.

www.ingramcontent.com/pod-product-compliance
Lightning Source LLC
Chambersburg PA
CBHW022132160426
43197CB00009B/1250